*Disneyland & Southern California
with Kids*

1998–1999

Disneyland
& *Southern California*
with Kids

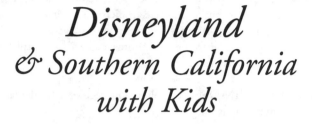

1998-1999

Carey Simon

Prima Publishing

PRIMA PUBLISHING and colophon are registered trademarks of Prima Communications, Inc.

Every effort has been made to make this book complete and accurate as of the date of publication. In a time of rapid change, however, it is difficult to ensure that all information is entirely accurate. Although the publisher and author cannot be liable for any inaccuracies or omissions in this book, they are always grateful for corrections and suggestions for improvement.

All products mentioned in this book are trademarks of their respective companies.

ISBN 0-7615-1242-X
ISSN 1083-2432

98 99 00 01 02 HH 10 9 8 7 6 5 4 3 2 1
Printed in the United States of America

How to Order
Single copies may be ordered from Prima Publishing, P.O. Box 1260BK, Rocklin, CA 95677; telephone (916) 632-4400. Quantity discounts are also available. On your letterhead, include information concerning the intended use of the books and the number of books you wish to purchase.

Visit us online at http://www.primapublishing.com

CONTENTS

PREFACE

I have been writing about family travel for a dozen years. Yet each time I return to a theme park, I am reminded just how confusing it can be for parents to visit for the first time with two young kids in tow and no idea of what to do first. This time around, however, I spoke to more and more families who realized the value of preparation. The parents I met who arrived at an attraction with a plan and knew that they probably couldn't see it all in a day were the ones who ended up having the most fun.

I was also reminded of how nice it is to discover things on your own—once you're armed with the basics. As long as your hotel is set, you know the best time to arrive at a theme park, and you have an idea of how you're going to tour it, you're ahead of the game. If you know in advance that not every ride in Disneyland will appeal to your kids or that Knott's Berry Farm can easily be toured in a day, you can relax and finally enjoy your vacation. Who knows, maybe your toddler will spot Tinkerbell flying from the Matterhorn, or perhaps at Sea World your daughter will learn why flamingos are pink. You might see Disneyland for the first time through the eyes of your 5-year-old or seize the opportunity to buy an ice cream, plop down on a bench, and just visit with your 12-year-old. After all, what are family vacations for?

I would like to thank James, William, Dana, Erin, Marlene, Gail, Brianna, Mark, Alex, Ardavan, and all the other children and parents I spoke with along the way who wondered why this woman was walking around the theme parks with a notebook in her hands when she could have been on the

Viper, Star Tours, or Windjammer. Thanks, too, to the parents I met from out of town—and from out of the country—and to the "seasoned" Southern California families I know who get to visit the theme parks whenever they want and all willingly shared their experiences and suggestions with me.

My daughter, Janey, has been assisting me with my research since she was 5 years old; even at 14 she still has a fresh view of the parks and activities. As usual, her commentary was invaluable. I am also appreciative to her friends Estee Zakar, Jamice Oxley, Amy Epstein, and Alison Kozburg for their sharp observational skills (and their lively companionship)—thanks for all your good work!

And thanks, of course, to Danny, who is always excited to accompany me to the theme parks!

WHAT MAKES THIS
GUIDE DIFFERENT?

Once upon a time, people with kids didn't travel. Couples lucky enough to have supportive relatives or nannies may have taken off now and then, leaving the kids behind. But more often families stayed home, figuring that geographic paralysis was the price of parenthood. Tour buses all over the world are filled with people in their sixties who deferred their dreams of Maui or Miami or Moscow until their kids were grown and out of the house.

Things have changed. No one is surprised anymore by the sight of an infant snoozing away in a four-star restaurant; not long ago, a letter to *Travel and Leisure* magazine inquired about the difficulty of locating Pampers in Nepal. Today, people take their kids everywhere—but some destinations stand out as nearly ideal for family travel. One of these is Southern California. Surrounded by beaches, mountains, and deserts and blessed with great weather and major attractions, the Los Angeles area is both exciting and overwhelming. This guide will help you cope with Southern California's wealth of vacation offerings. Although it focuses on Disneyland, it also supplies information on other area attractions, so you can choose which is most appropriate for your family.

Preplanning is essential—a two-hour wait that's merely annoying to a lone business traveler can be downright disastrous to a parent with hungry kids in tow. Nonetheless, some families try to wing it. You know the ones; you see them every morning at Disneyland, standing flat-footed in the middle of Main Street, babies bouncing in the strollers, toddlers wandering off in every direction, parents huddled over maps debating which attraction to see first. This approach is like trying to learn Lamaze after the contractions have begun.

To minimize problems and maximize fun while visiting a theme park, orient yourself before you arrive. By following the advice in this book, you'll learn to go against the crowds, zigging when everyone else zags so that you cut waiting time to a minimum and see twice as much as you would by drifting from queue to queue. The advice here is designed to fit the pace and pocketbook of those traveling with children, particularly children under the age of 10. The focus is on those attractions—like breakfast with the Disney characters—that first-timers can easily miss but that make all the difference to a character-struck toddler.

The basic rule when traveling with young children is to prepare without overscheduling. You want to be familiar enough with the layout of the park to find a restroom fast but not so driven that you have no time to rest and savor spontaneous pleasures. Fun stuff pops up all around Disneyland, but if you're grimly trying to make it from Fantasyland to Critter Country on schedule, you'll miss the very magic you've traveled so far to see.

No matter where you want to go on this vacation, or how many theme parks you think you'll visit, the one piece of advice you should follow is to *plan ahead.*

Keep in mind a few things as you read this book:

• This book focuses on children ages 3 and older.

• Although age-appropriateness is given for the rides at the major theme parks, you may have a very mature 7-year-old who loves roller coasters geared for preteens and teens or a 13-year-old who prefers to stay away from that type of ride.

• I have given suggestions for touring the parks, but every family is different. These suggestions are made to save time, but some families have the best time just taking what comes first.

• Some of the suggestions you'll read in the following pages are based on conversations with other people's children at the attractions, suggestions from kids who have bravely ridden the roller coasters I refused to go on, and comments from my own daughter and her friends.

• Because you never seem to have enough time or money on a vacation—particularly when with kids—I have included numerous tips for saving both. Throughout the book you will find the following three icons:

 money-saving tip

time-saving tip

helpful hint or tip

The three bugaboos of theme parks—the crowds, the exhaustion, and the expense—are especially tough on young families, and no amount of preplanning can totally eliminate them. After all, Disneyland can draw as many as 70,000 people a day, and it costs a family of four $130 just to park and get through the gate. You're going to get hot, get tired, and spend a lot of money—that's a given.

So why go at all? There's only one reason: Disney parks are the most fun places on Earth!

WHAT MAKES
DISNEYLAND SO
SPECIAL?

The answer to this question is, in a word, detail. The entire Disney fantasy is sustained through painstaking attention to detail.

True, the Disneyland rides are not designed to terrify, and kids accustomed to the monster coasters at other theme parks may find even Space Mountain tame. But if the attractions developed by the Disney imagineers don't rattle your molars, they do rattle your expectations. Consider a ride like Pirates of the Caribbean, in which Disney combines a catchy theme song and boat ride through eerie darkness with Audio-Animatronic figures so convincing that even the hair on the pirates' legs looks real. You emerge blinking into the sunlight of New Orleans Square 14 minutes later fully understanding why Disney insists its "rides" should be called "attractions."

The Disney theme parks are designed with the same precision that animators brought (and still bring) to the classic Disney films. Walt was such a perfectionist that he never let four frames per second suffice if eight were possible. The same sumptuousness is evident in Disneyland, which was the only one of the four Disney theme parks that he lived to see completed. (In addition to Walt Disney World in Orlando, Florida, Disney has parks in Tokyo and Paris.) California's Disneyland is smaller and more intimate than Disney World, and the park is full of nooks and crannies. At Disneyland you must be willing to meander, to take the path that seemingly leads nowhere. You'll be rewarded with small, unexpected pleasures, such as throwing pennies into the wishing well at the Snow White Grotto or pulling the sword from the stone and being declared ruler of all England. You might look up to see doves circling the Sleeping Beauty Castle or climbers scaling the Matterhorn at sunset.

The authors of some guidebooks seem immune to the Disney magic, which is why they can describe Dumbo as "a sporadically loading 10-unit cycle ride of the sort common to most midways" and advise you to pass it up. But it isn't only a sporadically loading cycle ride—it's Dumbo, and no 4-year-old worth her salt is going to let you pass it up. The special charm of Disneyland for us baby-boomer parents is that it's the theme park of our own childhood dreams. Once we pass through those gates, we all become 4-year-olds— impulsive, impatient, curious, easily duped, essentially cheerful, and ready to believe in magic.

PLANNING A
SOUTHERN CALIFORNIA
VACATION WITH KIDS

Southern California is made up of desert, ocean, and mountains. There is so much to see; if possible, you need to allow a week to 10 days for your trip. If you have less time, narrow your sites; one beach, one theme park, one zoo, and one museum should suffice. It's smarter to limit your choices than to try to see everything on a rushed schedule. Many of the attractions listed in this guide are as much as two hours away from each other—and Southern California traffic is, at best, unpredictable. The activities most appealing to families with young children often aren't in Los Angeles proper but in the surrounding innumerable small towns and beach cities. Don't underestimate the time you'll spend in transit. Be sure to read Chapter 2 for detailed information about airports, car rentals, and other transportation.

TRAVEL TIPS

• If you have a week or longer, plan to tour the area in sections. This means you'll be checking in and out of hotels more than once during your stay, admittedly a hassle with young children. But the alternative—long daily commutes from attraction to attraction—is even less appealing. A good plan is to organize your trip as follows:

Attractions in and North of Los Angeles. This includes Universal Studios, Magic Mountain, Hollywood, the Hollywood Wax Museum, the Los Angeles Zoo and Griffith Park, the La Brea Tar Pits, the Getty Center, the Natural

History Museum, the Peterson Automotive Museum, Beverly Hills, Santa Monica, and Malibu.

Attractions South of Los Angeles and in Anaheim. This includes Disneyland, Knott's Berry Farm, the Movieland Wax Museum, Medieval Times, Wild Bill's Wild West Show, Wild Rivers Waterpark, Long Beach, and ferries to Catalina Island.

Attractions in and Around San Diego. This includes Sea World, the San Diego Zoo, the San Diego Wild Animal Park, Balboa Park, Mission Bay Park, and the La Jolla beaches.

• When planning your day, cluster those attractions that can be done in one to two hours and are geographically close together. It may seem incongruent to visit Rodeo Drive, the La Brea Tar Pits, and the Hard Rock Café in a single day, but the sheer variety of experiences will keep the kids psyched—and, when you think about it, cultural incongruity is what Los Angeles is all about.

• It's always wise to pack light, but this can be a challenge in Southern California, where there may be substantial temperature variations throughout the course of a day. A family driving from Santa Monica to Magic Mountain can make the trip in an hour but may find that the temperature has climbed from the 70s to the 90s during the drive. Bring jackets for everyone (even in the summer), keep dressy clothes to a minimum, and try to find a hotel with guest laundry facilities.

HOTEL TIPS

• If you can only afford to pay $100 or less per night for lodging, you might think you're doomed to a no-frills chain. But clever families can stay at the Anaheim Hilton, the Sheraton Universal, or the San Diego Princess for the same rate you would expect to pay for a budget hotel. It's all in the planning. One strategy is to buy an Entertainment coupon book in your hometown before you leave for the trip or look into joining a travel club. Call early for reservations—only a certain number of rooms in each hotel is set aside for club members.

• Another option is to stay at your "splurge" hotel over the weekend. Many posh hotels, especially downtown, offer sharply discounted rates on Friday and Saturday nights.

• If you can travel off-season, you'll find substantial differences in hotel rates. Always ask about special promotions and packages. If your travel time is flexible, you might be able to take advantage of special promotions.

• Never accept the first rate offered—unless you're calling the Disneyland Hotel on a summer weekend! Rack rates, usually the first rate you're given, are the very top price. There are usually lower rates available. Ask whether the hotel offers corporate rates, AAA discounts, or, if you're traveling with grandparents, senior discounts.

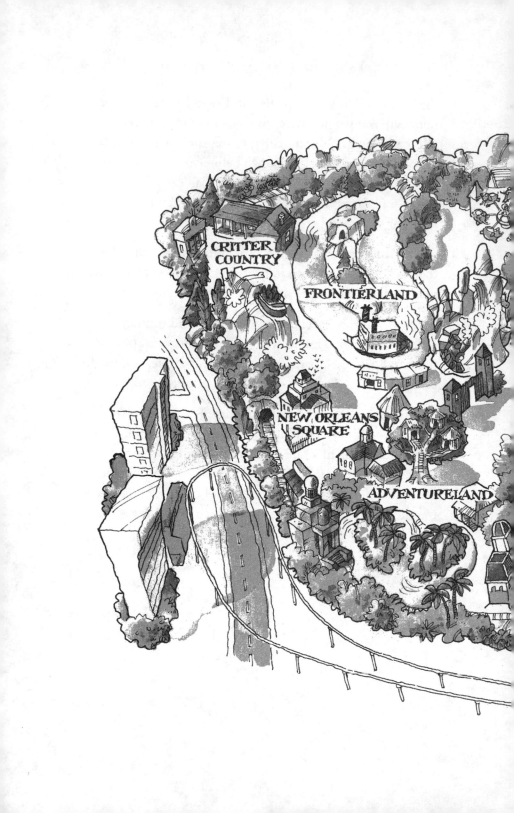

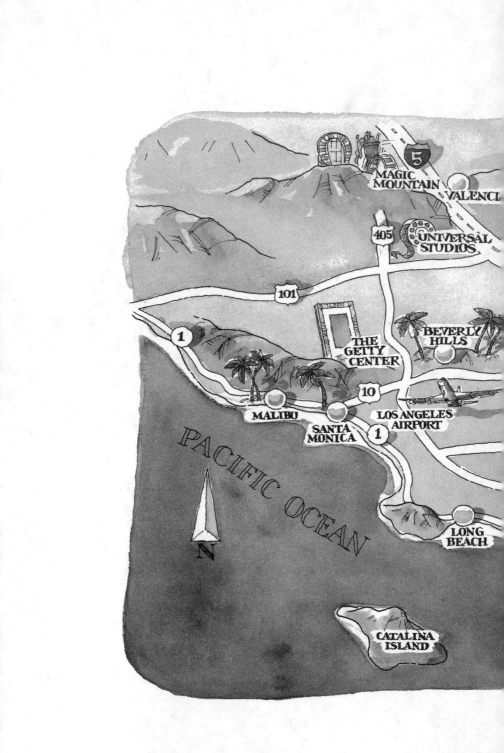

CHAPTER 1

Disneyland:
Before You Leave Home

WHEN TO VISIT

September through mid-December is the best time of year for families with young children to visit Disneyland. Crowds are light, the weather is pleasant, and many area hotels offer discounted rates.

There are disadvantages to a fall visit, of course. Some special parades and shows run only during the summer and holiday seasons. Disneyland closes earlier in the off-season, some weeks as early as 6 P.M., which is markedly different from summer, when it stays open as late as midnight. (In general, however, the early closing time should not deter you from a fall visit; you can board as many rides during an 8-hour day in October as you can during a 16-hour day in July.) You might also be reluctant to plan a trip during the school year. If you are, scan Chapter 11, Making the Trip Educational, for tips on how to make a vacation to Southern California more memorable and for ideas for school projects.

Although Thanksgiving, like all holidays, is crowded, the weeks between Thanksgiving and Christmas are a great time to visit Disneyland. The park is fetchingly decorated for Christmas with an enormous tree in the hub of Main Street, and holiday music wafts through the pine-scented air. We've visited the day before Christmas several years in a row—one year it's busy, the next it's not, and so on. Best of all, from late November to mid-December, the crowds are so light that you seem to have the park to yourself.

If you can't manage a fall visit, January through May is nearly as nice. With the exception of the holiday weeks around Presidents Day, Easter, and Memorial Day, spring crowds are much lighter than in the summer.

If you must visit in summer, the last two weeks in June are your best bet. Attendance and temperatures peak in July and August. The first week after Labor Day is good.

The absolute worst times are holidays. Christmas, Easter, and the Fourth of July pull in as many as 75,000 people a day, twice what you would find on a typical day in March. Extended hours can't compensate for the sheer volume of people, and popular rides develop two-hour lines. Even though special holiday parades and events are planned, you're far better off at home watching them on The Disney Channel. "Minor" holidays like Presidents Day, Labor Day, and Memorial Day are also poor choices; local families swarm the parks during the three-day weekends.

Because Disneyland draws so many people from the surrounding areas, weekends are always busier than weekdays. The least-crowded days are Tuesdays, Wednesdays, and Thursdays. Avoid Saturdays if you can.

Although it's not true that it never rains in California, the Anaheim area enjoys clear skies nearly year-round. December through March draws the most precipitation, but that shouldn't stop you. Travelers purchase ponchos at the Emporium and head for their favorite rides, where they find the lines have diminished substantially.

HOW LONG SHOULD YOU STAY?

It takes two full days to really enjoy Disneyland, largely because major attractions like Indiana Jones, Splash Mountain, Space Mountain, the new Tomorrowland rides, and the Matterhorn must be seen early in the morning if you wish to avoid lines. Even the most fleet-footed family would be hard pressed to see all the major attractions before

11 A.M, the time the park begins to fill. From that point on, the big rides will have long waits, and your touring will slow to a snail's pace. It's far better to have two mornings in the park; this allows you to visit all the biggies with relatively short waits and prevents you from trying to cram too much into a single day.

If your kids are young enough that you'll want to return to your hotel room for naps, buy the three-day passport. Three days are also needed by families determined to "do it all"—that is, to see every parade and show.

Tip: You don't have to use your two-, three-, and five-day passports on consecutive days; because touring Disneyland is tiring, consider breaking it up with a day at the beach.

Prices change often, so for updates call 714-999-4565. As this book goes to press, parking is $7 and preferred parking $12. The following admission prices are in effect:

5-Day Passport	Adult $63	Child (3–11)* $47
3-Day Passport	Adult $86	Child (3–11)* $65
2-Day Passport	Adult $63	Child (3–11)* $47
1-Day Passport	Adult $36	Child (3–11)* $26

Children under 3 are free.

If you really like Disneyland and are able to return within the year, consider an Annual Passport, which can run as low as $99 per person. Certain dates are blocked out, but it's still a clear source of savings for people who are true Disneyophiles.

Flex Passports (five-day) can be purchased by phone, at certain area hotels, at a Disney retail store, or online (www.disneyland.com). They not only offer a substantial discount—they also allow guests to get into Disneyland a full hour early on selected days. For families who want to stretch out their Disney experience—visiting the park on several days for just a few hours a day and spending the rest of the time lounging by the pool—the Flex Passports can't be beat.

If you're planning to see other attractions in the greater Los Angeles area, a rule of thumb is to allow one full day each to tour the following: Magic Mountain, Knott's Berry Farm, Universal Studios, Catalina Island, the San Diego Zoo, Sea World of San Diego, and the San Diego Wild Animal Park.

The following can be visited in half a day: the Los Angeles Zoo, any of the area beaches, the harbor cruises, Hollywood, Beverly Hills, and the La Brea Tar Pits.

The wax museums and family-style dinner shows like Medieval Times require only a few hours.

PHONE NUMBERS FOR PARK INFORMATION

• For a Disney vacation planning brochure, which gives information about hotel packages at Disney's hotels as well as other hotels in the area, call 800-225-2057.

• For general recorded information about hours, closed rides, special events, and so on for the day you visit, call 714-781-4565 or 714-999-4565.

• To speak directly to a representative and to order information for a future date that includes a vacation guide, park hours, a map of the park, an entertainment schedule, and ride opening and closing times, call 714-781-4560.

PHONE NUMBERS FOR ADVANCE TICKET PURCHASES, DISNEY DOLLAR PURCHASES, AND TOUR RESERVATIONS

• To order tickets by phone, call 714-781-4043 or write:

> Disneyland Ticket Mail Order
> P.O. Box 61061
> 1313 Harbor Boulevard
> Anaheim, CA 92803-6161

Be sure to include $8.50 extra for shipping and handling, but call first to verify that ticket prices are still valid.

Buying tickets in advance saves you from standing in line at the park, and because the price of tickets has been spiraling upward during the last three years, having tickets in hand guarantees you won't suffer if Disney decides it's time for an "adjustment." Be sure to ask whether any attractions will be closed for refurbishing or repairs during the dates you'll be visiting.

• You can purchase Disney dollars through Disneyland Guest Relations (714-781-4565). These bills come in denominations of $1 (Mickey), $5 (Goofy), and $10 (Minnie) and are accepted in place of regular currency throughout Disneyland and the Disneyland and Pacific Hotels.

In addition to being great fun, Disney dollars can be a cost-saving tool. Some wily parents purchase Disney dollars in advance to be used for snacks and souvenirs and then manage to convince their kids that this is the only type of money the park accepts. When the Disney dollars are gone, the spending stops.

- Disneyland offers an educational three-hour package that is packed with mind-blowing trivia (such as how many gallons of water it takes to fill the Submarine Lagoon) and visits six rides with the guide. The tour is enjoyable for kids 7 and older; most of the information will be lost on kids younger than that. The price is $48 for adults and $36 for kids 3 to 11, which includes full-day admission to Disneyland. After the tour is over, you'll have time to explore the park on your own. If you'd like to take the tour and you're going in a busy season, make reservations in advance by calling Guest Relations at 714-781-4565.

THINGS TO DISCUSS WITH YOUR KIDS BEFORE YOU LEAVE HOME

Your kids should be as informed and prepared as you are, so you may want to discuss the following points with them before the vacation begins.

The Trip Itself

If you're coming from out of town, there are two schools of thought on how far in advance of the trip you should tell the kids about it. Because many families make vacation plans six months in advance or more, it's easy to fall into a "waiting for Christmas" syndrome, with the kids in a lather of anticipation weeks before you leave. To avoid the agony of a long countdown, I know of parents who packed in secret, woke the kids up at five one morning, and announced, "Get in the car, we're going to Disneyland." Probably the best method is somewhere between the two extremes. Tell the kids you're going at the time you make your reservations, but don't begin poring over the maps and brochures in earnest until about two weeks before the trip.

Height Requirements

Get out your yardstick, because if your kids fall under the
height required for riding Indiana Jones (46 inches) or
Space Mountain, Splash Mountain, the Matterhorn, or Big
Thunder Mountain Railroad (all 40 inches), you should
break it to them now. Disney vigilantly enforces these
requirements, and there is nothing worse than queuing up,
only to have little Nathan ejected unceremoniously just as
you approach the ride.

The Layout of the Park

Kids 7 or older should have some idea of the layout of the
park. If you're letting preteens and teens roam about on
their own, definitely brief them on the location of major
attractions.

Among the families surveyed for this book, there was a
direct correlation between the amount of advance research
they had done and how much they enjoyed the trip. Visitors
who show up at Disneyland without any preparation can
still have fun, but their comments were sprinkled with
"Next time I'll know . . ." and "If only we had . . ."

The pleasures of being prepared extend to preschoolers.
If you purchase a Disneyland coloring book or a few
Viewmaster reels to enjoy on the way to Anaheim, even the
youngest child will arrive able to identify the Swiss Family
Robinson Treehouse. A little knowledge prior to entering
the gate helps you decide how to best spend your time and
eliminates those whadda-we-do-now debates.

The Classic Stories of Disney

If your children are under 7, another good pre-trip purchase is
a set of Disney paperbacks with audiotapes. Even though

parental eyes may glaze over as Dumbo rewinds for its three-thousandth straight hearing, these tapes and books help to pass the time and familiarize kids with the characters and rides they'll be seeing once they arrive. (If you find kiddie tapes too annoying, bring along a Walkman for the kids to use.)

Souvenirs and Money

Will you save all souvenir purchases for the last day? Buy one small souvenir every day? Are the children expected to spend their own money, or will Mom and Dad spring for the T-shirts? Whatever you decide depends on your pocketbook and your interpretation of fiscal responsibility—but do set rules before you're in the park. Otherwise, the collection of goodies will lure you into spending far more than you anticipated.

DON'T LEAVE HOME WITHOUT . . .

✓ Comfortable shoes. This is no time to be breaking in new Reeboks.

✓ A lightweight jacket. California evenings can be cool, even in the summer.

✓ Minimal clothing. Many hotels have guest laundry facilities, and you can always use Woolite to wash things out in the sink. Many families make the mistake of overpacking, not figuring in all the souvenirs they'll be bringing back. Disney T-shirts are not only great for touring but can serve as swimsuit cover-ups and sleepwear as well.

✓ Sunscreen. Keep a tube with you and apply it often. Sunburn is the number one complaint at the first-aid clinic, and the nurses there report they see the worst cases in the fall and spring. Don't let a cool day trick you into forgetting your sunscreen.

✓ Disposable diapers, film, blank camcorder tapes, and baby formula. All these are available within Disneyland, but at prime prices.

✓ Juice boxes. They are handy while flying or driving to Anaheim, and you might also want to keep several on hand while touring. Young kids can become dehydrated rapidly.

✓ A waist pouch or fanny pack. It's a good alternative to dragging along a purse while touring and frees up your hands for boarding rides, pushing strollers, and holding on to your kids.

✓ Sunglasses. The California sun is so blindingly bright that more than once I've reached for my sunglasses only to realize I already had them on. Kids too young for sunglasses need wide-billed caps to cut down on the glare.

✓ Strollers. Either bring your own or rent one at the park for $7. If you're staying at the sprawling Disneyland Hotel or one of the other large resorts, you'll need a stroller just to get from the pool to your room. Families planning to walk back and forth between their hotel and Disneyland will find it nearly impossible to cross the enormous parking lot without a stroller. A backpack-style carrier is also helpful because it lifts babies up to the eye level of adults and enables them to see all the action.

Tip: Think about renting a stroller for at least part of the day if you have a child around 4 or 5 who may rebel against being pushed in the morning but will collapse from exhaustion by early afternoon. The rental fee is well worth it.

✓ Credit cards. You can use credit cards to purchase theme park tickets, souvenirs in the larger shops, and food at sit-down restaurants. The Bank of Main Street, located on Main Street, will cash checks and give cash advances on credit cards.

CHAPTER 2

Disneyland: Settling In

GETTING TO DISNEYLAND

Disneyland is located in Anaheim, which is *not* a suburb of Los Angeles, as many out-of-towners think. Actually, Anaheim is a city in Orange County, and it is located approximately one hour south of Los Angeles International Airport (LAX). Because the greater Los Angeles area and Orange County are actually a network of small and not-so-small towns, and the attractions mentioned in this book may be as much as an hour-and-a-half drive from each other, it is impractical to rely on public transportation to tour the sites. Most tourists fly into LAX and rent a car at that airport, where a huge selection is available and rates are from $150 to $250 a week with unlimited mileage.

If you decide to rent a car, make reservations in advance by dialing one of the numbers that follow. If you need car seats for the kids, request them at the time you make your reservation.

Many car companies will ask you to buy collision damage waiver insurance (CDW), which can dramatically up the price of your rental. If you belong to AAA or have an inclusive policy on your car at home, you might not need to purchase CDW. Likewise, some credit cards offer automatic CDW coverage if you pay for the rental with that card. Be sure to check these possibilities before you leave home because you might be able to dodge this expense.

AREA RENTAL CAR COMPANIES

Alamo	800-327-9633
Avis	800-331-1212
Budget	800-527-0700
Dollar	800-421-6878
Hertz	800-654-3131
National	800-227-7368
Thrifty	800-367-2277

From LAX, drive south on I-405 (the San Diego Freeway), east on Highway 22 (the Garden Grove Freeway), and then north on Harbor Boulevard, which runs directly past Disneyland. A book of area maps or a AAA guide can be your best friend in Southern California. Guest Services at your hotel is also a good source of street directions. Many hotels offer maps that outline the routes to the major theme parks and beaches as well as the travel time each takes. Car rental companies also provide maps. Just make sure the one you're using is current.

If you are going directly to Disneyland from the airport, you can save money by taking a shuttle from LAX to your Anaheim hotel. These are not hotel shuttles but commercial shuttles that pick up and drop off passengers at a variety of locations. Many of the area hotels offer transportation to Disneyland, and you can easily do without a car during your days there. Call a car rental company and ask for the Anaheim locations; many of the large hotels have a rental booth inside their lobbies, and you can pick up a car on your last day at Disneyland and then move on to the rest of your vacation. This trick saves you not only the money you'll fork over to rent a car that will sit unmoved in the hotel parking lot for several days but also the steep parking fees, which can add up over your stay.

If you're going to take a shuttle from the airport to your hotel, reserve it in advance. It is frustrating indeed to land at LAX after a long flight and then be forced to camp on a curb with the kids for an hour while reserved shuttles zoom by.

Try the SuperShuttle (800-258-3826 or 213-775-6600), which costs $13 per person and serves many Anaheim hotels (but doesn't have car seats), or the Airport Bus (800-772-5299 or 714-938-8900) at $14 for each adult, $8 for kids 3 to 11. A taxi can be an expensive option—cab fees between

LAX and Anaheim can run as high as $85—but worth it if you're arriving at a very late hour or have several people in your family.

LAX is the largest and best-known of the area airports, but it isn't the only way to fly into Southern California. It might not even be the best way. Some airlines offer direct flights into John Wayne Airport in Orange County or into Long Beach Airport, both located just south of Los Angeles and closer to Anaheim and Disneyland.

If you're planning to make San Diego part of your vacation, consider flying there first. Although the San Diego airport offers numerous direct flights to cities all over the United States, it is nowhere near as large and overwhelming as LAX. Tour the zoo, Sea World, and other area attractions first, then head north to Anaheim and Los Angeles.

ANAHEIM HOTELS: WHAT TO EXPECT IN EVERY PRICE RANGE

The area around Disneyland is full of hotels, ranging from the enormous Anaheim Hilton, with every amenity imaginable and a price tag to match, to the Magic Lamp and Lantern, twin motels at a budget price.

Four major roads flank Disneyland. Harbor Boulevard is the busiest, and most of the hotels located there are mid-priced, in the $85 to $150 range. The hotels on Katella Avenue are smaller, older, and for the most part cheaper. West Street is taken up primarily by the mammoth Disneyland Hotel and Disneyland Pacific Hotel. The fourth road, Ball Street, is not recommended—it's a rundown area just off I-5, adjacent to the service entrances of Disneyland, making the main entrance too far to walk to. Convention Way, which runs between the convention center and Harbor Boulevard, is home to some of the more expensive resort-style hotels in the area, such as the Anaheim Hilton.

To get a complete listing of area hotels and a general visitor's guide, call or write:

Anaheim/Orange County Visitor and Convention
    Bureau
Dept. OVG
P.O. Box 4270
Anaheim, CA 92803
714-999-8999 or 888-598-3200 (toll free)

The official visitor's guide is evenhanded, listing lots of hotels and giving few recommendations. In an area where rates range from $40 to $200 a night and where the elegant and the unsafe can literally be found within a block of each other, finding a hotel suited to your needs will take some research. Following are some ideas of what you can expect in each price range. The hotels listed are at the very least clean, safe, and within walking distance of Disneyland. When rates are given, remember that these are "rack rates"—the highest nondiscounted rates the hotels offer. By calling the local 714 numbers at the hotels, you can ask about special packages or off-season rates. Be sure to read the section "Hotel Tips" in "Planning a Southern California Vacation with Kids" at the beginning of this book for more ideas on saving money.

Over $150 per Night

At about $200 a night, the Disneyland Hotel and the new Disneyland Pacific Hotel next door are in a class by themselves. They are the most expensive hotels in the area, but in exchange for your money you get entertainment, sports, character breakfasts, on-site shows, unbeatable proximity to

Disneyland via the monorail, and that great intangible—an atmosphere that's pure Disney. The Pacific Hotel offers great amenities, a less frenetic atmosphere, and use of all the Disneyland Hotel's extras. Guests at both hotels can arrange to have theme park tickets waiting for them when they check in and are entitled to purchase five-day Flex Passports, which cost the same as a two-day passport. Guests can also take advantage of Magic Mornings, when they are allowed to enter the park before the general public.

Disneyland Hotel

1150 West Cerritos Avenue
714-956-6400

Staying at the Disneyland Hotel, which offers monorail service directly into the heart of Disneyland and a tram to the front gate, is very convenient. But rates run between $180 to $215 a night. (Sometimes packages drop the rate during the off-season.) The advantage to staying at the Disneyland Hotel is that it's a full-fledged resort with a manmade marina and remote control tugboats, pedal boats, arcades, four pools (including one with its own sand beach), and a waterfall so enormous that you can walk beneath it through a special passageway. The location is unbeatable, the grounds are absolutely lovely, and hotel guests are allowed into the park a full hour-and-a-half ahead of the other guests on Early Admission Days. The best Disney merchandise store in town is in the hotel, and you can choose between eight different eateries, ranging from the casual, kid-pleasing Monorail Café to the swank Granville's Steak House.

Goofy's Kitchen, which serves a wildly popular buffet breakfast each morning ($14.50 for adults, $8.95 for kids

4 to 12, $3 for kids under 4), also offers the chance to meet four to eight Disney characters who visit with the kids and stop for pictures, autographs, and hugs. If breakfast isn't your thing, the characters also appear at a buffet dinner from 5 to 9 P.M. ($18 for adults, $8.95 for kids 4 to 12, $3 for kids under 4), with a salad bar, choice of entrées, and a to-die-for dessert bar. It takes at least 40 minutes for all the available characters to work the room, so plan for a leisurely meal.

The Disneyland Hotel is a 24-hour hub of activity. It's fun to end the day by visiting the huge, brightly colored koi fish that swim in the pool beneath the waterfall. Or have a cone at the ice cream galley, then try your hand at the remote-controlled cars on the Off-Road Raceway. Parents can relax at the wine bar or hear live music in one of the lounges. There's a rowdy family-style saloon show complete with line dancing at the Neon Cactus (be sure to check ahead—we had to leave by a specified time with our under-21 kids) and the nightly Fantasy Waters music and light show down by the "beach." The show is free.

Of course, many of these amenities can be enjoyed by Disneyland visitors who are not guests of the hotel. Anyone is free to take the monorail over to the hotel for lunch, rent a pedal boat, or watch a presentation of Fantasy Waters. Likewise, the character buffets and Neon Cactus shows are open to all. But it's undeniably more exciting to have all this happening in your backyard. One mother, whose children vary considerably in age, reported that ordinarily her pre-teens would have howled in protest when she forced them to return to the hotel in the afternoon so the baby could nap. But the Disneyland Hotel had so much going on that the older kids could amuse themselves for hours while the younger one slept.

Speaking of sleeping: The rooms vary in size and view depending on which tower they're in. I liked the rooms in Bonita Tower the best. Remember, the earlier you check in (especially in summer), the better chance you have to request a large room and get it. Rates *begin* at $180 in summer. But remember that the rates are based on availability—if the hotel is booked, it's doubtful a $180 room will be available.

Disneyland Pacific Hotel

1717 South West Street
714-999-0990

This refurbished high-rise hotel is located just next door to the Disneyland Hotel. It's more of a boutique hotel and a good choice if you want the amenities offered by the first but want to sleep in a less frenetic atmosphere.

The Pacific has one pool and two restaurants, one of which, the PCH Grill, offers a great character breakfast buffet. This one's even more interactive than the one at the Disneyland Hotel. The characters sing and dance and even stop to sit with the kids. The cost is the same as at the Disneyland Hotel ($14.50 for adults, $8.95 for kids 4 to 12, $3 for kids under 4). If you're not looking for a full breakfast, you can take coffee and snacks up to your room from the lobby coffee bar. Or if you want to splurge, reserve your room on the Concierge Level, where you'll get morning breakfasts, afternoon drinks and snacks, and sodas all day in a private lounge, and free use of the workout facilities.

Currently, you'll need to either walk to the monorail or tram next door or request a free ride from the bell captain. Eventually, the hotel will provide a tram just out the back door.

Standard rooms at the Pacific are quite comfortable and are decorated with interpretive Disney art, reading chairs that pull out to a single bed (or a sofa bed in some rooms), and spacious closets. Rooms on the concierge level come with coffeemakers and VCRs and the amenities already noted.

Getting a bit tired of roaming Disneyland? There's a special treat at the Pacific Hotel that will allow you to take at least one afternoon off. The hotel offers "Practically Perfect Tea," where you won't find a single sign of Mickey. Instead, Mary Poppins and other characters from the movie pop in for a spot of tea and a chat. Try it for morning tea (and breakfast); in the afternoon the tea is called "A Spoon Full of Sugar." Be sure to check with the front desk for days and times, and definitely make reservations in advance, as it's quite popular. The price is steep ($18.50 for adults, $12.50 for kids), so make sure little Jane or Michael will sit through it.

$100 to $150 per Night

In this price range, expect resort-style amenities such as a pool area with a café or bar and hot tub, other sports such as tennis or an exercise center, and possibly a kids' program. A higher-priced hotel will offer a direct shuttle to Disneyland (and perhaps other area attractions) and possibly an airport shuttle as well. A variety of on-site restaurants should also be available, ranging from a casual coffee shop where you can take the kids to more elegant dining suitable for parents' night out.

Anaheim Hilton

777 Convention Way
800-445-8667 or 714-750-4321

The Hilton's kids' program is called Vacation Station. The hotel provides a lending booth stocked with games, books, and toys for kids 2 to 10. Children also receive free gifts at check-in and get a behind-the-scenes hotel tour (seeing the laundry room is a popular event). The program is available daily from Memorial Day to Labor Day weekend. The fitness center (for adults) is huge—there's even a basketball court!—and the restaurants provide children's menus. As in all Hiltons, children of any age sleep free in their parents' room. Be sure to ask about special packages.

Hyatt Regency Alicante

At Harbor and Chapman
800-233-1234 or 714-750-1234

The Hyatt has a wonderful away-from-it-all quality because of its location a few blocks down from the Disneyland main gate—but the shuttle buses that run every 30 minutes mean that you can still get to the action fast. The concierge can help arrange in-room evening babysitting, and the kids are given special frequent-stay cards at check-in.

The Hyatt offers discounts on weekends that sometimes drop the rates significantly.

Best Western Park Place Inn

1544 South Harbor Boulevard
800-854-8175 or 714-776-4800

This relatively new hotel offers minisuites, king-size beds, and hideaway sofas and a full-service restaurant.

$50 to $100 per Night

Most of the hotels in the Disneyland area fall into this price range. For this rate you should have a direct shuttle to

Disneyland, an on-site coffee shop, a guest laundry room, a game room, and a decent-size pool.

Many area hotels also offer a Flex Passport, which allows you early entrance to Disneyland on selected days and substantial discounts. (For example, five days for $63 for adults, $47 for kids 3 to 11.)

Candy Cane Inn

1747 South Harbor Boulevard
800-345-7057 or 714-774-5284

In an area not known for ambiance, the Candy Cane Inn stands out on the basis of pure physical appeal. The rooms are bright and airy even though they face the parking lot or pool. A few rooms face flower-filled gardens, but you must request one in advance. Only 250 feet from the main gate of Disneyland, the Candy Cane is a good choice for families wanting to pay under $100. There's a year-round shuttle to the park and numerous packages that include other Southern California theme parks. Deluxe rooms with two beds can also fit a crib *and* a roll-away. There's a complimentary breakfast buffet, a heated swimming pool, a children's pool, and laundry facilities for guest use. The deluxe rooms have microwaves and refrigerators.

Tip: This is one of the best bets in the $50 to $100 range.

Best Western Anaheim Inn

1630 South Harbor Boulevard
800-854-8175 or 714-774-1050

Of all the Best Westerns in the area, this one is the closest to the Disneyland gates. Expect refrigerators and coffeemakers in every room, an on-site restaurant and guest laundry room, shuttle service, and value packages that include theme park tickets and some meals. Although some rates for a family of four are under $100, they are by availability only. Expect to pay around $110 on a busy week or weekend.

Carousel Inn and Suites

1530 South Harbor Boulevard
800-854-6767 or 714-758-0444

This hotel puts you right across the street from the "happiest place on Earth." The Carousel Inn offers rooms for around $99 and suites at $99 to $160 as well as packages that include tours and tickets to area attractions. The hotel is especially cheery and bright, and all rooms with two queen-size beds feature a microwave, coffeemaker, refrigerator, and hair dryer. Free continental breakfast is served in an exceptionally charming breakfast room, and a large heated pool is located on the roof.

 Tip: The rooms in the back are bigger and quieter.

Castle Inn

1734 South Harbor Boulevard
800-521-5653 or 714-774-8111

This funky-looking place, complete with turrets, spires, and heraldry, has in-room refrigerators, a guest laundry room, a large pool area, some suites, and on-site car rental. The rooms are dark but clean, and there's room for a crib and a roll-away. Expect to pay about $88 for a unit with two queen-size beds.

Inn at the Park

1855 South Harbor Boulevard
800-353-2773 or 714-750-1811

One of the few high-rises in the area, the 500-room hotel has all the standard amenities and an Olympic-size swimming pool. Kids stay free.

Jolly Roger Hotel

640 West Katella Avenue
800-446-1555 or 714-772-7621

The Jolly Roger's 237 rooms and suites are set in three buildings, and there's a restaurant, lounge, two large pools, room service, and direct shuttles. The accommodations are roomy and provide space for a crib or roll-away. Be sure to ask about their Kids Eat Free Program. However, because it's on Katella instead of Harbor the rooms are a bit lower priced than many other hotels offering similar amenities. Rates start around $60 and move up to $100 on the busiest days and holidays.

Anaheim Plaza

1700 South Harbor Boulevard
800-228-1357 or 714-772-5900

Although the Anaheim Plaza is another large hotel, the rooms are spread out over 10 acres. This hotel, which is actually the closest to the Disneyland entrance, has an Olympic-size pool, direct shuttles, a guest laundry room, and an exceptionally complete restaurant. A limited number of units have balconies or patios, but all the rooms are bright and comfortable. Expect to pay anywhere between $89 and $110 for a room with two double or two queen-size beds.

Park Inn International

> 1520 South Harbor Boulevard
> 800-828-4898 or 714-635-7275

The medieval-looking building is attractive, and the grounds are very well kept. The Park Inn features a terrace-level pool (where you can watch the fireworks at night), a game room, a guest laundry room, shuttles to both Disneyland and area airports, and a refrigerator in every room. Rates range from $80 to $100.

Desert Inn and Suites

> 1600 South Harbor Boulevard
> 800-433-5270 or 714-772-5050

Paying just a little more gets you a suite, complete with living room area and minikitchen consisting of a micro-wave and a refrigerator. Standard rooms come with two queen-size beds, whereas the Desert Suites can accommodate families as large as 10. Be sure to ask for a nice bright room—some units are very dark. The hotel also features an indoor pool and whirlpool, free continental breakfast, and a rooftop sunning deck, which is also a good place to watch the evening fireworks display at Disneyland. Standard rooms are well priced under $100; naturally, suites cost more. But for a family of eight, the rates run $90 to $150.

Ramada Inn Maingate

1460 South Harbor Boulevard
800-447-4048 or 714-772-6777

The Maingate is a large hotel with many amenities, including a guest laundry, a nice-size pool, and free continental breakfast. Rooms come in several configurations, so let them know your needs, and they'll try to accommodate you. You can get in-room refrigerators or microwaves on request. Right out in front is a food court with pizza and other food items to take back to the room.

Less Than $50 per Night

If you're not picky about atmosphere or amenities, it's possible to find a hotel quite close to Disneyland for less than $50 a night. At this price you're talking about a small fenced-in pool, cinder-block buildings, and no restaurant. You'll have to either share a shuttle with other small hotels (which means a longer commute time) or walk.

Magic Lamp Hotel

1030 West Katella Avenue
800-422-1556 or 714-772-7242

Basic rooms run about $40 a night. There's a guest laundry room on the premises and an outdoor pool.

Magic Carpet Motel

1016 West Katella Avenue
800-422-1556 or 714-772-9450

A cousin to the Magic Lamp, the Magic Carpet also offers a pool and the same rates. But you can get kitchenettes here, and two units have three double beds.

Others
In the immediate area, there are also Travelodges (800-578-7878) and Days' Inns (800-325-2525), which are usually under $50.

THINGS TO ASK
WHEN BOOKING A HOTEL

Even among hotels in the same general price range and area, there can be a real difference in the level of services offered. The following questions should help you sniff out the best deal.

✓ Does the hotel provide shuttle service to Disneyland? Are the buses express, or do they stop and pick up riders at other hotels? How often do they run? How early and how late do they run? Is there any charge?

   Ideally, your hotel shuttle should begin running at least an hour before Disneyland opens, enabling you to get there early and take full advantage of the less crowded morning hours. Also, the hotel should run shuttles well after the park closes. At closing time a swarm of people exit at once, and it can take as long as an hour to get down Main Street, through the gates, and out of the parking lot. If your shuttle service shuts down at the exact hour the park closes, you'll be forced to leave along with everyone else and get caught in the crush. However, if your shuttle runs later, you can spend a few minutes browsing the shops or eating at the restaurants on Main Street, which stay open about an hour after the park's official closing time. This is essential if you'll be visiting in the off-season, when the park closes at 6 P.M. During these weeks you have to contend not only with the crowds leaving Disneyland but also with Anaheim rush-hour traffic.

Tip: Many hotels point out that they are located so close to Disneyland that walking is an option. But if you have very young kids, regard this information skeptically. The hotels may indeed be located within a few blocks of the park, but trekking across the 100-acre Disneyland parking lot with small kids is a major hassle in the morning and downright unsafe in the evening, when cars are racing for the exits. It's nice to have the option to take the shuttle, especially in the evenings, when you're exhausted.

✓ Do kids stay free? Up to what age?

This is a crucial question. Some hotels let kids stay free until they're 21, but others charge 12-year-olds an extra $15 a night. Ask whether the kids-stay-free plan exists just for existing beds or whether there is an extra charge for a roll-away or crib.

✓ Does the hotel provide a free buffet or continental breakfast? Is there a coffee shop? If not, what fast-food or family-style restaurants are nearby?

✓ Does the hotel have any suites with kitchens?

No one is suggesting that you spend your vacation cooking, but some Anaheim hotels have villa-style lodgings, and if you can prepare cereal and sandwiches in the room, you'll save significant bucks. If a hotel has, at the very least, a microwave and a refrigerator, you won't have to worry about preparing baby food.

✓ Is there airport pickup? Shuttle service to other area attractions? What's the charge?

✓ Is there a charge for parking?

✓ Does the hotel have a kids' club? For what ages? When does it run? Does it run only in summer? What are the activities? Is there a charge?

Don't expect many children's programs in Anaheim. Most hotels expect that, because there is so much to do nearby, you won't need facilities other than swimming pools to keep the kids occupied. However, you might find that a hotel has a game room or, in the case of the Anaheim Hilton, a lending desk for toys and books. The other exception is the Disneyland Hotel with its numerous activities.

✓ Can arrangements be made for in-room babysitters? If so, what are their qualifications? The cost? How far in advance should you reserve a sitter if you want an adult evening out?

✓ Is there a guest laundry room on the premises?

✓ Does the hotel offer a Flex Passport or any other price breaks on tickets? Are tickets to Disneyland and other area attractions available through Guest Services? Are the tickets discounted? (Just being able to purchase your tickets at your hotel prior to arriving at Disneyland can save you loads of time.)

✓ Is there on-site car rental?

✓ Does the hotel offer any packages?

Tip: Some of the larger hotels put together their own deals, often including breakfasts and discounted tickets. It never hurts to ask.

STAYING ON-SITE VERSUS OFF-SITE

Consider staying at either the Disneyland Hotel or the Pacific Hotel if any of the following conditions apply:

✓ You're going during the summer or a holiday season.
   If you're visiting during a busy time, you'll need every extra minute, so staying on-site is worth the cost.

✓ You'll be visiting for only a day or two.
   Likewise, if your visit is short, you can't afford to waste much time commuting, so staying in a hotel located a mere 10-minute monorail ride from Space Mountain helps you see as much as possible as fast as possible.

✓ You have young kids who will need to return to the hotel midday for a nap.
   The monorail makes it easy to get back fast.

✓ You won't have a car with you.
   Being without wheels is a snap at the Disneyland (or Pacific) Hotel, which has both the monorail and express trams running at all hours as well as handy bus access to area airports.

✓ There will be times when your party will split up.
   Will Dad be taking the younger child back for a rest while Mom stays in the park with the older one? Do you have a late-rising 13-year-old who would like to

meet the rest of you inside the park at 10 A.M. each morning? The convenience of the monorail lets each of you go your own way on your own schedule.

But staying on-site isn't for everyone. Consider an off-site hotel if:

✓ You're trying to save money.

Make no mistake—both the Disneyland Hotel and the Pacific Hotel are considerably more expensive than other area hotels.

✓ Your kids eat a lot.

Food is far more expensive at the Disneyland Hotel than at the fast-food places along Harbor Boulevard. Off-site hotels also sometimes offer free breakfasts, which you won't get at the Disneyland Hotel.

✓ The trip is spur-of-the-moment.

The Disneyland Hotel fills up in advance during peak seasons.

✓ You plan to spend lots of time at other area attractions.

It's silly to pay top dollar for proximity to Disneyland if you're headed for Knott's Berry Farm or Sea World. (Some families stay one or two nights at the Disneyland or the Pacific, then move to a less expensive hotel for the days they aren't doing Disneyland.)

✓ You want peace and quiet at the end of the day.

A couple of families reported that there was simply too much going on at the Disneyland Hotel and that they couldn't get the kids settled down for naps or bedtime. If you want to avoid that sleeping-in-the-middle-of-a-theme-park feel, you may be better off at the Ramada. However, you should consider the quieter Pacific Hotel if your budget permits.

SHOULD YOU BUY A PACKAGE?

This question is a toughie. There are advantages to package trips, the most notable being that it's possible to save money. It's also helpful to know up front what your vacation will cost. Packages often require hefty prepayments, which are painful at the time, but at least you return home knowing how much you've spent.

Package trips can also have drawbacks. As with buying a fully loaded car off a dealer's lot, you may find yourself paying for options you don't want or don't need. Be doubly wary of the very cheap packages put together by travel agencies or those advertised in the Sunday papers. If a deal sounds too good to be true, it often is.

Disney Packages

The Walt Disney Company, which is still the largest of the package companies for Disney Resort vacations, offers several different packages, some with lodging at the Disneyland Hotel and others that board you at another nearby hotel. You can tailor your package to your needs and add on trips to San Diego, Catalina, or other Los Angeles area attractions. For a brochure detailing the packages, call or write:

Walt Disney Travel Company
P.O. Box 4180
Anaheim, CA 92803
714-520-5050

Off-Site Hotel Packages

Several of the larger hotels in Anaheim offer their own packages, which in general include lodging, breakfast, theme park tickets, and in some cases car rental. When you call a hotel to check rates or request a brochure, be sure to ask whether packages are available.

Travel Agents

Travel agents can help you compare hotel prices and are often savvy about airfare and car rental discounts as well. Some agency packages can save you money, but beware if an agent offers an extremely low rate on a hotel. As noted, there's a huge variation in the quality of Anaheim lodging, so a simple assurance that "It's really close to Disneyland" means nothing. If the hotel the agent recommends isn't listed in this book, check it out by requesting a brochure.

Also, be leery of the all-day tours often included in agency packages; they're often impractical for families with young kids. One family surveyed for this book recounted a horrific tale about a package so inclusive that it even offered a jaunt to Mexico. They happily signed up and were then forced to drag their two preschoolers through a 16-hour marathon of bus riding and touring with no way to get back to the hotel room. Some agency packages can be a good deal, but the moral is to ask lots of questions so you know what you're getting into.

MAGIC KINGDOM CLUB

If your family is really dizzy for Disney, it makes economic sense to join the Magic Kingdom Club. Joining is as easy as dialing 800-56-DISNEY, or 800-563-4763; the price is $65 for a two-year membership. Perks include:

- 10% discounts on rooms at the Disneyland Hotel

- Discounts of up to 25% at selected hotels at Walt Disney World in Florida

- Special packages to both Disneyland and Walt Disney World

- 10% discounts on merchandise purchased at Disney Stores worldwide or items ordered from the Disney Catalog

- Reduced ticket prices to both Disneyland and Walt Disney World

- 10% dining discounts at a wide variety of Disneyland eateries

- Up to 30% discounts at National Car Rental

- Special vacation packages

- Discounts and packages to Disneyland Paris and Tokyo Disneyland

A family visiting Disneyland or Walt Disney World will find that club membership pays for itself several times over. Once you have your membership gold card in hand, you'll be able to book rooms and purchase packages by dialing a special number.

WHERE TO EAT IN ANAHEIM

There are numerous fast-food restaurants up and down Harbor Boulevard, but several stand out as good ones for family sit-down dining.

• Tony Roma's (714-520-0200), across from the Disneyland entrance, has a reasonably priced children's menu along with good-size portions of chicken, ribs, and hamburgers for everyone else.

• Belisle (714-750-6560), across from the Hyatt Alicante, is especially good for breakfast. Although the prices aren't cheap, the portions are huge.

• The Spaghetti Station (714-956-3250) is good for— what do you think?

• Acapulco Restaurant (714-956-7380) serves up mild, hearty Mexican dishes and is always welcoming to families.

CHAPTER *3*

Disneyland:
Tips and Touring Plans

You've finally made it to Anaheim and are all unpacked and ready to go. Now what?

• On the evening you arrive in Anaheim, dial 999-4565 or contact the Guest Services desk at your hotel for the next day's opening time. If you learn, for example, that Disneyland is scheduled to open at 9 A.M., be at the gate by 8:30. Sometimes, for no apparent reason, the gates open early. This is a gift from the gods, and you should be prepared to capitalize on it. You can ride a dozen attractions while the other 50,000 poor saps are still out on Harbor Boulevard.

• Come early! This is one of the most important pieces of advice in the entire book. By beating the crowds, you can not only visit attractions in quick succession but also avoid the parking and transportation nightmares that occur when the park fills to peak capacity around 11 A.M.

For families with young kids, it's especially important to avoid the exhaustion that comes with just trying to get there. If you're staying off-site, it can take a full hour from when you leave your hotel to when you board your first ride, which is enough to shatter the equanimity of even the best-behaved kids. They've been waiting for this vacation a long time and flying and riding a long time. You owe it to them to get into the park fast.

• Even if the park doesn't open ahead of the stated time, guests are frequently ushered into the Main Street section of the park early. This means you can get maps, strollers, and entertainment schedules; window-shop; visit with the characters who frequently hang around Town Square in the morning; select a muffin from the Blue Ribbon Bakery; and still be at the ropes blocking the end of

Main Street by 9 A.M., far ahead of the throngs outside the main turnstiles.

• New attractions, like the new Tomorrowland, are always hot, and the thrill rides, like Space Mountain and Splash Mountain, are eternally popular. Plan to see these either early in the day, late at night, or when a big event, such as one of the parades, siphons off other potential riders.

• Eat at "off" times. Some families eat a light breakfast, then have an early lunch around 11 A.M. and dinner at 5 P.M. Others eat a huge breakfast, then have a late lunch around 3 P.M. and a final meal after the park closes. (If you tour late and are really bushed, many area hotels offer in-room pizza delivery.) The key is to avoid restaurants during the peak dining hours.

• Be aware that kids usually want to ride their favorites more than once. Parents who overschedule to the point where there is no time to revisit Splash Mountain risk a mutiny.

One way to handle this is to leave the last evening of your trip free as "greatest hits" time, so that everyone can visit his or her personal favorite once more. If you feel like lugging the camcorder around only once, make this the day.

• Use the touring plan to cut down on arguments and debates. It's a hapless parent indeed who sits down at lunch and says, "What next?" Three kids will have three different answers. If you have a basic plan and stick with it, you'll cut down on indecision, wandering in circles, and bickering.

• If you're going to be at Disneyland for two days or longer, plan to visit the most popular attractions on different days. Many families arrive determined to take in Space

Mountain, Splash Mountain, Indiana Jones, Star Tours, and Pirates of the Caribbean their first day, then end up spending hours in line. Better to see a couple of biggies during the first hour after the park opens. After that, move on to less popular attractions, saving the other biggies for subsequent mornings.

• If you leave the park and plan to return, save your stroller receipt and get your hand stamped. You can reenter swiftly by showing your ticket and stamped hand, and you won't have to pay again for a new stroller. (Don't worry if you're leaving to go back to your hotel pool for a swim— the hand stamps are waterproof.) Likewise, if you have a car, save your parking receipt so you won't have to pay the $7 fee more than once.

• One excellent way to break up a long touring day is to take the monorail to the Disneyland Hotel for lunch. The restaurants there are far less crowded than those within Disneyland, adults can order alcohol if they like, and the hotel is a fun destination in itself. A few minutes spent driving the remote-controlled cars or boats can be a welcome respite from the crowds within the park, and the monorail ride from Tomorrowland to the hotel is far faster than taking a shuttle bus or walking to the other hotels.

The Monorail Café is the restaurant closest to the monorail station, with a Mickey-mask kiddie menu and a funky fifties decor. Another good bet is the character breakfast or dinner buffet at Goofy's Kitchen; or have an early lunch around 11 A.M. or an early dinner around 5 P.M. to effectively break up a long day of touring.

• Don't worry if your child doesn't meet the height requirement and you and your spouse want to ride an attraction. Just ask the attendant for a "child switch" pass, which lets one of you ride while the other stays with the child. When your spouse is done, just show your pass to the attendant and switch with your spouse.

TIPS FOR VISITORS STAYING AT THE DISNEYLAND HOTEL

• If your kids are poky in the morning, one parent should pick up juice and muffins at the Monorail Café and bring them back to your room. This allows you to eat while you dress. Service takes forever at the Disneyland Hotel restaurants, and room service is so slow that you should forget it altogether, at least on the days when you're trying to get an early start in the park.

• There are two ways to get to Disneyland from the Disneyland Hotel: by tram and by monorail. Both rides take less than 10 minutes, and both the trams and the monorail load fast and run frequently. The only real difference between the two is that the tram lets you out at the front gate (outside Main Street) and the monorail stops in Tomorrowland. To ride the monorail, you need your ticket. You can buy tickets in advance at the monorail station, which saves you time and allows you to avoid the main gate altogether.

If it's one of the mornings when hotel guests are allowed in an hour early, take the tram. On other mornings, it's a toss-up. The monorail doesn't begin to run until closer to the stated opening time, but because it lets you out deep within the park, you'll miss the mobs coming down Main Street.

Tip: There is no stroller rental in Tomorrowland, so if you're in desperate need of a stroller, you must take the tram to the front gate.

• On Magic Mornings, when hotel guests are allowed early entrance, take the tram to the main gate and look for the special entrance to the extreme right near Guest Relations. Head for Indiana Jones first, then Splash Mountain.

• You should definitely return to the hotel for lunch. If the kids are really exhausted, pick up salads or sandwiches at Maxie's Pantry and take them to your room so that you can eat and rest simultaneously.

• During the summers and holidays, Disneyland runs very long hours. You'll combat the crowds most successfully by touring in the morning, then returning to the hotel in the afternoon. Eat dinner at the hotel and reenter the park around 7 P.M. You should be well rested, the crowds will have thinned, and the kids may surprise you by lasting past the 11 P.M. parade.

• If you purchase anything while in the park, you can have the package delivered directly to your hotel room. It beats dragging around a stuffed Dumbo all day.

TIPS FOR VISITORS STAYING OFF-SITE

• Many hotels either serve a free continental breakfast or have coffee shops where you can pick up sweet rolls and juice, which you can take back to your room and eat while you prepare to go. There are also several fast-food places along Harbor Boulevard where you can pick up a McMuffin or some McVersion of breakfast on the run. Eat lightly now, and you'll be ready for lunch by 11 A.M. and thus in a good "food pattern" to avoid the long waits that occur at peak dining hours.

Another effective food pattern is to rise early and get a good, solid breakfast at one of the buffet family-style restaurants, which provide maximum food for minimum price. Then you can snack through lunch and have an early dinner.

• Ideally, your hotel tram will begin to run an hour before the stated park opening time, so you can be at the main gates and have your tickets purchased ahead of the crowds.

• If your kids are so young that they need to nap, you may have no alternative but to return to your hotel at some point during the day. Hotel trams run less frequently midday than they do in the morning and evening. Get a tram schedule from your hotel so you won't end up standing on the asphalt for 30 minutes while the kids whine.

Should you be visiting during the off-season, when the park closes early, it would be too time-consuming to make the commute four times. Instead of attempting to return to your hotel, consider stopping at one of the "Afternoon Resting Places" listed in Chapter 4.

• It may seem logical to make your purchases in the evening as you leave the park, but everyone else has the same idea, and the stores are mobbed then. Shop in early afternoon, when the rides are crowded, and then either take your loot back to the room when you return for your midday break or, if you're not planning to leave the park, stow your purchases in one of the lockers on Main Street (around the corner from the Market House) or outside the exit turnstiles and retrieve them in the evening.

• Staying all day? California can be cool in the morning, hot in the afternoon, and cool again at night, as hundreds of shivering, sunburned kids watching the 11 P.M. parade can attest to. Dress in layers, so that you can adapt your clothing to the changes in temperature.

YOUR FIRST HOUR IN DISNEYLAND

Nowhere do the Disney people exhibit more whimsy than in their opening policy. Call 999-4565 the day before you plan to visit and confirm hours of operation. Then be at the gate 30 minutes early.

Once through the gate, stop for a second to visit with the characters at Town Square but try to be at the end of Main Street by the stated opening time, when the ropes drop.

Head straight toward Adventureland. Ride Indiana Jones first, then continue left toward Splash Mountain in Critter Country. Then go to Frontierland and Big Thunder Mountain Railroad. Admittedly, these three start the day with a bang, but you'll face long lines if you wait past 10 A.M. to ride them.

Tip: If you'll be at Disneyland for more than a day, head toward Tomorrowland on your second morning. Ride Space Mountain, Star Tours, the new Tomorrowland rides, and then the Matterhorn in Fantasyland.

If your kids are too young for these major rides, head straight down Main Street and through Sleeping Beauty Castle to Fantasyland. There you will be greeted by that most lovely of all Disneyland sights: riderless Dumbos and teacups for the taking. You should be able to board seven or eight rides within the first hour you arrive.

Tip: It's important to keep moving during this crucial first hour of the day, when you can do so much so fast. If there's a huge gap in the age of your kids, consider splitting up. One parent can take the toddlers to Fantasyland, the other can take the ride-warriors to the major coasters, and you can meet up again in an hour.

YOUR LAST HOUR IN DISNEYLAND

If you're visiting during the on-season, your objective should be to watch the evening parade and fireworks without being caught in the mass exodus of people who head out the gate just after the last float passes. If the parade is coming from Main Street, your strategy should be to watch from near the Town Square hub. Turn in your strollers, take a final bathroom break, or buy any last-minute trinkets while you're waiting. Once the parade passes, head toward the exit. As some of the first people to see the parade, you'll also be among the first to get out the gate and board the tram. If the parade is coming from Toontown, your strategy shifts. Don't try to go down Main Street toward the exits after the parade passes—you'll simply be following the parade route along with thousands of other people. Kill a little time by stopping for a snack or shopping, and exit by way of Main Street after about 20 minutes, when the parade crowd will have begun to disperse.

If you stayed to watch Fantasmic! or the fireworks, stop for a snack or browse in the shops after the show is over. It takes about 30 minutes for the crowd to disperse.

Touring in the off-season? When there is no final parade or show and the park closes as early as 6 P.M., you risk exiting in the middle of Anaheim's rush hour. This is no big deal if you're headed for the Disneyland Hotel or you walked over, but it can be a real mess if you're parked in the parking lot. Main Street stays open an hour after the rest of

Disneyland closes, so if you line up for dinner at one of the Main Street restaurants about 30 minutes before the park closes and linger over your meal, you'll be exiting behind the main surge of people. There's *no* reason to rush toward the gates at 6:01.

HOW TO CUSTOMIZE A TOURING PLAN

There's no substitute for a good touring plan. The trick is to modify the generic touring plans in guidebooks, tailoring them to your family's specific needs. For example, if your kids are big fans of the Disney characters, you may end up spending hours in Toontown. On the other hand, if no one in your group likes anything remotely scary, you can cross off certain attractions from your list from the start.

In creating a personalized touring plan, the first step is to use the map in this book (or the more detailed Disney map, assuming you've had the foresight to call 714-781-4560 and request one in advance) to familiarize yourself with the basic layout of Disneyland. Getting to Splash Mountain early is considerably easier if you know where Splash Mountain is. The second step is to poll your family on which attractions they most want to see, then build these priorities into the plan.

The third step is to divide each day of your visit into three components: morning, afternoon, and evening. You don't have to specify where you'll be every hour—that's too confining—but it's helpful to have some sense of how you'll break up each day. If you're going during the on-season, when the park runs long hours, or you have very young kids, you may opt to break up the day by returning to your hotel room. But if you have only one day, or if you're going during the off-season, when the park closes early, think about switching gears in the afternoon, taking in theater-style presentations after lunch when the kids need a breather.

One key to traffic flow is the newness of the attraction. Disneyland draws a lot of locals who may have ridden an old standard like the Jungle Cruise a dozen times but who will head straight for the new stuff the minute they hit the park. In time, undoubtedly, even Indiana Jones will become old hat to L.A. residents. But in the meantime, it's still hot. Once Tomorrowland opens, the crowds are sure to head there first, leaving Indiana Jones to you.

Tip: Forget trying to see things in geographic sequence— a mistake many first-time visitors make. In order to pack it all into a single day, it's better to make three laps of the park. Consider the morning lap to be your biggies cycle, when you'll attempt to board the most popular rides before the park fills up. In the afternoon, look for either passive attractions that let you sit a bit, like the Country Bear Jamboree, or high-capacity attractions that load swiftly even when the park is packed, like Pirates of the Caribbean. Finally, in the evening make your wrap-up lap, visiting any of the biggies you missed in the morning or focusing on attractions like the Haunted Mansion or Dumbo, which are especially atmospheric in the dark.

That's a lot of walking, you say? Sure it is, but the alternative is to spend a lot of time in lines, which is ultimately harder on the legs—and the nerves—than the three-lap plan.

Note: You'll notice that this book occasionally provides alternative suggestions for kids 7 and younger and those 8 and older. Obviously, this is an arbitrary division; some 5-year-olds are daredevils who scoff at Space Mountain, and some 10-year-olds get queasy on the teacups. You're the best judge of what your own child can handle. For specifics about the various rides, their scare factors, and height requirements, see Chapter 5.

To get a general idea of what to see when, scan the following lists.

Biggies (Good Choices for Morning)
    Indiana Jones
    Splash Mountain
    Big Thunder Mountain Railroad
    Matterhorn
    Space Mountain
    Star Tours
    New Tomorrowland attractions

For younger kids, the major Fantasyland rides (Dumbo, Peter Pan's Flight, and so on) qualify as biggies because they board slowly and huge lines build in the afternoon. Also, for younger kids, the Tomorrowland Autopia and Submarine Voyage can get really jammed after lunch.

Good Choices for Afternoon
    Country Bear Jamboree
    Pirates of the Caribbean
    It's a Small World
    Enchanted Tiki Room
    Swiss Family Robinson Treehouse
    Tom Sawyer Island
    Big Thunder Ranch
    Rivers of America boats
    The railroad
    The monorail
    The afternoon parades

Good Choices for Evening
Anything you missed from the biggies list, especially the
Fantasyland rides
Jungle Cruise
Haunted Mansion
Toontown
Fantasmic!

A DETAILED
ONE-DAY TOURING PLAN

For families with only one day to do all of Disneyland, the
task is challenging indeed.

Morning
1. Be at the front gate at least 30 minutes before the stated
   opening time. Be at the end of Main Street by the time
   the ropes drop.
2. Veer sharply left at the end of Main Street and head first
   to Indiana Jones in Adventureland.
3. Go left as you exit and continue through New Orleans
   Square to Critter Country. Ride Splash Mountain.
4. As you exit, head left again, toward Big Thunder
   Mountain in Frontierland.
5. After Big Thunder Mountain, head toward Fantasyland. Ride the Matterhorn, then any other Fantasyland
   attractions that catch your fancy.
6. Have a late breakfast or early lunch and catch your
   breath.

Afternoon
1. Ride Pirates of the Caribbean.
2. Watch the Country Bear Jamboree.

3. Choose one of the three Rivers of America watercraft and/or spend an hour touring Tom Sawyer Island. If your kids are younger, go to Toontown instead and let them play among the interactive exhibits and visit the characters' houses.
4. Walk through the Swiss Family Robinson Treehouse.
5. If the Jungle Cruise line is 30 minutes or less, ride it now. If the wait is longer, save it for evening.
6. Ride It's a Small World.
7. Return to Main Street for the parade. Browse the shops and have a snack.
8. This is the hottest and most crowded time of the day. If the park is open late, consider leaving for a couple of hours.

Evening

1. Go to Toontown. The lines for Roger Rabbit's Car Toon Spin and Gadget's Go Coaster will be much shorter now.
2. Head toward Tomorrowland. Ride the Submarine Voyage, the Tomorrowland Autopia, and other new Tomorrowland attractions.
3. During the first evening parade, ride Star Tours and Space Mountain. The lines get shorter when everyone moves toward Main Street.
4. Cut back toward Fantasyland and ride anything you missed earlier in the day.
5. Go to New Orleans Square and tour the Haunted Mansion.
6. Return to Main Street for the final parade.
7. If it's showing, watch Fantasmic! over Rivers of America in Frontierland.

It probably makes you exhausted just to read the one-day plan. If your kids are young, prepare to miss quite a few attractions. Read the ride descriptions in Chapter 5 to help you determine what's a must-see for your family and what's skippable. But even after you make your deletions, still follow the plan as closely as possible—it's designed to keep you moving against the crowds and to help you hold the time you'll spend standing in line to a minimum.

A DETAILED
TWO-DAY TOURING PLAN

Two days allow you to relax the pace a little.

Day 1—Morning
1. Be through the gates 30 minutes early and at the end of Main Street by the time the ropes drop.
2. Ride Indiana Jones first, then move on to Splash Mountain and Big Thunder Mountain Railroad.
3. Move on to Fantasyland and ride any attractions that appeal to your kids.
4. Walk back to New Orleans Square. Ride Pirates of the Caribbean, then have lunch at either the Blue Bayou Restaurant, Café Orleans, or the French Market.

Day 1—Afternoon
1. After lunch, enjoy the shops of New Orleans Square. Then return to Critter Country and see the Country Bear Jamboree.
2. Visit any Frontierland or New Orleans Square attractions that catch your eye.

3. Leave the park and return to your hotel for a break. (Families heading out the front gate will want to be off Main Street well before the afternoon parade. It's a mob scene.) If it's the off-season and the park closes early, take a ride on the railroad or go to Tom Sawyer Island.

Day 1—Evening
1. Either eat before you reenter the park or, if you decided to stay in the park, eat an early dinner at one of the buffeterias.
2. Go to Tomorrowland and ride any Tomorrowland attractions that catch your eye.
3. Cut across Main Street to Adventureland. By now, crowds should be forming for the first of the evening parades, meaning shorter waits at the Jungle Cruise and Haunted Mansion. Ride them now or, if you missed them earlier, ride Splash Mountain or Pirates of the Caribbean.
4. Have a snack and be back on Main Street in time to stake out curb space for the second run of the evening parade.

Day 2—Morning
1. If your kids are young, start the day with an early character breakfast at Goofy's Kitchen at the Disneyland Hotel or at the PCH Grill in the Pacific Hotel.
2. Catch the monorail from the hotel to Tomorrowland. (If you want to make lunch reservations at the Golden Horseshoe, one parent should slip away and make them within an hour after entering the park.)
3. Ride Space Mountain.
4. Ride Star Tours.

5. Ride the Matterhorn.
6. Visit any Fantasyland attractions you missed the first day.

Day 2—Afternoon

1. Visit the characters and enjoy the rides and games of Toontown.
2. Line up for your lunch at the Golden Horseshoe.
3. Ride It's a Small World.
4. See the afternoon parade.
5. Either exit the park for your midday rest or, if it's the off-season and you plan to stay in the park, catch the train from Toontown to New Orleans Square.

Day 2—Evening

1. If you left the park for a midday break, eat an early dinner outside the park. If you stayed in the park, eat at the Golden Horseshoe Jamboree, which offers a dinner show, or at Big Thunder Barbeque.
2. After dinner, ride anything you missed earlier and revisit favorites.
3. See Fantasmic!

IF YOU HAVE THREE DAYS OR MORE

If you have three days or more, follow the basic two-day plan, adding extras at your leisure. Take in special shows, let the kids try out the arcades and shooting galleries, or spend more time in Toontown or on Tom Sawyer Island. Visit the Disney Gallery in New Orleans Square, take the three-hour guided tour, and visit Innoventions in Tomorrowland.

Families with Flex Passports, which allow them up to five days of touring, report that this is a very low stress way to see Disneyland. They can go in each day for only two to three hours in the morning and ride whatever they want with little waiting. Other families use the pass primarily at night, when the park is fetchingly lighted and far less crowded. "We lie by the pool all day," one father wrote, "and only enter Disneyland for a couple of hours at a time. That's really the way to see it. The kids are well rested and thrilled by everything."

THINGS YOU DON'T WANT
TO THINK ABOUT

Disneyland might be the most fun place on Earth, but the unexpected can occur. The best plan is to be prepared.

Lost Children

Obviously, your best bet is not to get separated in the first place. Savvy families have standard meeting spots. Because everyone designates Sleeping Beauty Castle or the Matterhorn as their meeting spots, those places are always mobbed. Plan to catch up with your crowd at a more out-of-the-way locale, like the benches in Critter Country or the Main Street Cinema.

Consider pinning your child's name, your name, and your hotel or home phone number to a piece of his or her clothing. You may be surprised, but your 2-year-old may know you only as "Daddy" and not realize your name is Tim! You may see families all dressed in the same bright T-shirts (maybe your hometown Little League team's name), so that youngsters can better spot their parents in a crowd. As the woman in charge of the Lost Children center said to me, "Imagine. When you're little, all you see are legs! After a while, all those legs begin to look alike to a small child." Although many parents don't believe in using harnesses (those leashlike apparatuses that attach to toddlers' chests), it may be something to consider if you have an especially active toddler.

If you do get separated and your kids are too young to understand the idea of a meeting place, act fast. The Lost Children center is inside the first-aid clinic on Main Street. Disney employees are well briefed about what to do when they encounter a lost child, so the odds are good that if Jeremy has been wandering around alone for more than a few minutes, he has been intercepted by a park employee and is on his way to the Lost Children center. In real emergencies (the child is very young or handicapped or doesn't turn up within 15 minutes or so), all-points bulletins are put out among employees. So if you lose a child, don't spend half an hour wandering around. Contact the nearest Disney employee. Sometimes kids are so interested in what's going on around them that they don't look upset or lost and thus no Disney employee notices them. Explain to your kids that if they get separated from you, they should look for someone with a Disney name tag. The employee can then report to the Lost Kids Desk, and the attendant there can tell you where the child is.

Rain

Go anyway. Short of an all-out monsoon, most Disneyland attractions are open as usual and crowds are thin. If you get caught in a cloudburst, rain ponchos are available in the larger shops. Although hardly high fashion, they're better than trying to maneuver an umbrella through crowds, especially if you're also pushing a stroller.

Injuries and Illnesses

There's a first-aid clinic on the right side (as you enter) of Main Street that is staffed with registered nurses. Although the clinic treats most of its patients for maladies like sunburn, motion sickness, and minor boo-boos, it can also handle major emergencies and, when necessary, provide transport to an area hospital. The nurses at the clinic drew raves from the families surveyed for both their efficiency and their gentleness with teary kids.

Closed Attractions

Because Disneyland is open 365 days a year, it refurbishes and repairs the rides as needed. Thus, at any given time several attractions may be closed for maintenance, and it can be heartbreaking if an attraction your family highly anticipated is closed. The best bet is to call 714-999-4565 before you leave home to find out which rides will be off-line during the week you're visiting. There's still a slight chance that a ride will malfunction during your visit and be closed temporarily, but the Disney people are so vigilant about maintenance that this happens very rarely.

Auto Breakdowns

If you return to the parking lot at midnight to find your battery dead or your tire flat, walk back to the nearest tram stop. The lot is patrolled continually by security people who can call for help. By far the most common problem is forgetting where you parked. Be sure to write down your row number as you leave your car in the morning. Although "Tinkerbell 83" may seem easy to remember at 8 A.M., you may not be able to retrieve that information 16 mind-numbing hours later.

Running Out of Money

The Bank of Main Street gives cash advances on credit cards and refunds on lost traveler's checks. You can also cash personal checks for small amounts with proper ID and exchange foreign currency. The bank is open from 9 A.M. to 4 P.M., even on weekends. The Versateller outside the main turnstiles can handle your needs in the evening.

BARE NECESSITIES: DIAPERS, STROLLERS, AND OTHER DETAILS

Traveling with kids, with people with special needs, or when pregnant requires advance planning. But if there is one place that is prepared for any visitor, it is Disneyland.

Diapers

Diapers can be purchased at the Stroller Shop, the Baby Services Center, and the Emporium on Main Street. Changing tables are available in all the women's restrooms and—finally!—in most men's rooms. If a father has trouble locating a well-equipped men's room, he can always use the Baby Services Center.

Baby Services Center

Children's rockers, microwaves for heating bottles and baby food, high chairs, and changing tables are all found at the newly redecorated Baby Services Center near the lockers on Main Street. Diapers, formula, bottled water for babies, and jars of baby food are for sale. There are also kid-size toilets, so this is a good place to bring a toddler who is being potty trained.

Breastfeeding

Disneyland is casual and family oriented, and many mothers nurse in the theaters and restaurants. Some of the shows, like Great Moments with Mr. Lincoln, are dark, quiet, and ideal for nursing. Others are so loud that the baby may be distracted. If you prefer more privacy, try the Baby Services Center. While mom takes a private room, siblings can play in the small enclosed play area in the Center.

Strollers

If you'll need a stroller every day, bring your own from home. It's a rare occurrence, but strollers do get stolen, so you may prefer to rent. And if you have an older child who will need a stroller for only part of the day (say in the afternoon when he or she is napping), rental isn't a bad option. The rental fee is $7. The stroller rental stand is to your right just after you enter the main gate. There is no rental stand near the monorail entrance. If you leave the park for a midday break, keep your receipt so you can get a new stroller without paying again when you return. Tie something like a bandana or a balloon to your stroller to mark it to reduce the probability that someone will swipe it while you're inside Peter Pan's Flight. As one mother observed, "Otherwise honest people seem to think nothing of stealing a rented stroller but stop when they see they might be taking a personal possession as well."

Stroller stolen anyway? Return to the stroller rental desk with your receipt in hand and you'll be issued a new one without having to pay again. Tinkerbell Toy Shoppe in Fantasyland can also replace a stolen stroller.

Special Needs

Call Guest Relations at 714-999-4565 weeks in advance and request a copy of the Disneyland Disabled Guest Guide to familiarize yourself with the location of ramps and special entrances. Most attractions are accessible by wheelchair, although some, like Space Mountain, require riders to walk a few steps. Attendants will be happy to help guests board and disembark from rides. Guests in wheelchairs are frequently boarded through their own gates and thus often can avoid waiting in line altogether. Wheelchairs can be rented at the stroller rental stand near the main entrance. This is not a bad idea if you're traveling with an older person who, although not technically handicapped, may have difficulty walking through a long day. Portable tape players and cassettes for sight-impaired guests are available, as are volume-control telephones for the hearing impaired. Check at Guest Relations for free use of this equipment.

If you're traveling with a person who has special needs, relax. Disneyland is one of the most frequently requested destinations of Make a Wish and other such charities, and park employees are accustomed to dealing with a variety of situations, even those in which the child is very seriously ill. A lot of thought has gone into how to make the attractions safe and accessible for these kids, and if you make the Disney employees aware of your presence and your needs in advance, they will help you any way they can.

Changing Clothes

Southern California has two seasons—day and night—and if you'll be touring for 16 straight hours, you'll need to dress in layers. (This is especially important if you'll be riding

Splash Mountain; when you emerge from the ride dripping wet at 8 A.M. or 10 P.M., you'll need to either shed your top layer of clothing or change T-shirts.) Jackets and sweaters can come off midmorning, but it will get chilly again at night. Either get a locker or tie your outer layers around your waist as the temperature climbs. We've often used a change in the weather as a good excuse to buy that Pooh sweatshirt or Disneyland T-shirt, and we make that one of the souvenirs of the trip.

Charging Privileges

American Express, MasterCard, and Visa are accepted for tickets, merchandise in the larger shops, and food at the buffeterias and sit-down restaurants. Many large area hotels, including the Disneyland and the Pacific, allow guests to charge food and amenities to their rooms with a resort ID card, which saves you from having to take your wallet by the pool or having to constantly dole out cash to the kids. But if you opt to get an ID with charging privileges for a child, impress on him or her that the card should be treated like a credit card and is not an open invitation to purchase all seven stuffed dwarfs from the hotel gift shop or, heaven forbid, to obtain cash advances. And although there is no complete consensus about this, be sure your child has a picture ID if he or she is using the hotel card. Some spots require it, but some don't ask for it.

If you lose your resort ID, report it immediately to the front desk to avoid unauthorized charges.

Pregnant?

A few precautions are in order.

Make regular meal stops. Instead of buying a burger from a vendor, get out of the sun and off your feet at a buffeteria or sit-down restaurant. Be sure to drink lots of fluids, as dehydration is a real danger. Throw an extra juice box into your tote bag for emergencies.

If you aren't accustomed to walking three to four miles a day (an average Disneyland trek), begin to get in shape at home by starting a walking regimen several months before your trip.

Standing stock-still can be much more tiring than walking, so let your husband stand in line for rides. You and the kids can join him as he enters the final turn of the queue.

The wilder rides are off limits to pregnant women; use this time to rest on a nearby bench. The Baby Services Center is also a good place for mothers-to-be to take a break.

This is definitely an occasion when it's worth the money to stay at the Disneyland or the Pacific Hotel. Return to your room in midafternoon and put your feet up.

Don't forget to check out restroom locations in advance.

SAVING TIME

Here are some helpful tips for making the most of your time at Disneyland.

- Do as much as you can before you leave home. Purchase theme park tickets and reserve rental cars and hotel rooms long before you pull out of your own driveway. Every call you make now is a line you won't have to stand in later.

- Visit the most popular attractions before 11 A.M. and after 9 P.M.

- Eat lunch either at 11 A.M. or after 2 P.M. You can save both time and money by making lunch your big meal of the day.

• Be aware that once you cross into the Anaheim city limits, there is an inverse relationship between time and money; you have to be willing to spend one to save the other. A well-located hotel may cost more, but if it saves you commuting time, it's worth it.

• If you have only one day to tour, it's imperative that you go during the off-season if you can. You can see in one day in November what would take three days in July.

• Don't feel you have to do it all. If you study this guide before you go, you'll realize that not every attraction will be equally attractive to your family. Disneyland won't come to an end if you skip a few rides.

• Restaurant service can be very slow. If you're on a tight schedule, stick to fast food while in the park and order a pizza at night when you get back to your hotel room.

SAVING MONEY

Saving money at Disneyland is somewhat of an oxymoron, but there are ways to contain the damage.

• You can cut lodging costs by buying an Entertainment book in your hometown or joining a travel club. These books, which sell for $35 to $50, are best known for their restaurant discount coupons, but they also contain a nationwide list of hotels that offer 50% discounts to cardholders. Price breaks like these are invaluable to a family staying at one of the larger hotels or resorts.

• A Magic Kingdom Club card entitles you to discounts on hotels, meals, tickets, and merchandise (for details, see Chapter 1).

- Eat as many meals as possible outside the park.

- If you do want to try one of the nicer Disneyland restaurants, go at lunch, when prices are far lower than at dinner. And remember that restaurant portions are huge, even for kiddie meals. Consider letting two family members share an entrée.

- Except for maybe an autograph book and a T-shirt, hold off souvenir purchases until the last day. By then the kids will really know what they want, and you won't waste money on impulse purchases.

- Buy your film, camcorder tapes, diapers, and sunscreen at home before you leave. These things are available within Disneyland, but you'll pay dearly for the convenience.

- If you're staying near Disneyland, you might not need a rental car for the Anaheim part of your vacation. There are local car rental booths (many inside hotels) where you can pick up a car as you leave town and head for other California locations. Most area hotels offer shuttle service to Disneyland, and some have service to Knott's Berry Farm as well.

- A character breakfast can set you back $50, so if your budget is tight, concentrate on other ways to meet the characters.

- Look for hotels that offer the Flex Passport, a money-saving way to experience Disneyland, or purchase your tickets in advance (see Chapter 1).

CHAPTER 4

Disneyland:
All the Little Extras

DINING TIPS

There are lots of places to eat at Disneyland, but the following are the best choices.

Best Breakfasts

The character breakfasts are a time-honored Disney tradition and not without reason. Between five and eight characters circulate among the diners, stopping for nice long visits
and plenty of pictures. Younger kids, who may have been
trampled by the crowds in earlier attempts to give Minnie a
hug, adore these breakfasts, and older children frequently
get into the spirit, too. You can visit either Goofy's Kitchen
at the Disneyland Hotel or PCH Grill at the Pacific Hotel
next door, where Minnie is joined by Bell, Gaston, and
Merlin for magic and songs. During summers and holidays,
the Plaza Inn on Main Street and the Tomorrowland Terrace
feature character breakfasts. Call 714-999-4565 to verify
times and prices; in the on-season, you can also make
reservations.

It's a good idea to schedule your character breakfast on
the last morning you visit. The characters are very large, and
toddlers are often a bit intimidated at first. But after they've
been in the park for a while, little ones have had a chance to
warm up to the characters and usually aren't as frightened.
Also, if you wait until the morning you're leaving, you won't
be rushing to get to the park, and the character breakfasts
are a nice send-off for the trip home. Several families surveyed, whether guests at the Disneyland Hotel or not, said
they ate at Goofy's Kitchen on their last morning in Anaheim, then checked out of their hotel and headed for the
airport. If the children have had their character breakfast

already yet just can't get enough of Mickey, take them for Mickey Mouse pancakes at the River Belle Terrace in the park.

Best Dining Bets

Best bets at the Disneyland Hotel include the conveniently located and casual Monorail Café and the buffets at Goofy's Kitchen. Next door at the Pacific Hotel, the PCH Grill has pleasant, quick service and a catchy decor. The staff will let the kids make their own pizzas with the chef.

Service at the sit-down restaurants within Disneyland is agonizingly slow. Let's face it, this is hardly five-star dining, so there's no reason you should wait 30 minutes for a chicken salad sandwich. Families with only one day in the park should skip the sit-down restaurants. Even the fast-food lines can make you antsy—the wait at Critter Country's Hungry Bear Restaurant was also 30 minutes.

Disneyland has several buffeterias, which are cafeterias with a limited selection. Because you push your own tray through and the service lines move at a steady clip, the buffeterias are a good choice when you just can't face another burger but you don't have the time or the patience for an hour-long meal. Try the River Belle and Casa Mexicana, both in Frontierland, or the French Market or Café Orleans in New Orleans Square. The buffeterias are also good choices for picky eaters because you can see the food before you order and the menu choices are listed at the door.

Disneyland offers $4 kids' meals at sit-down restaurants all over the park. Each restaurant serves a different variation, but menus are always posted at the door.

Do *not* eat between noon and 2 P.M. or between 6 and 8 P.M. If the kids are collapsing from hunger, hold them off with a snack. And never eat in Fantasyland, which is mobbed all day. Choose Tomorrowland or New Orleans Square instead.

If you want to try one of the nicer Disneyland eateries, make it the romantic Blue Bayou, which is located inside Pirates of the Caribbean and is so dark that you'll dine by candlelight at 11 A.M. The Blue Bayou is cheaper at lunch (but still expensive), and you won't sacrifice any atmosphere by going in the morning. As you sit among the trees dripping Spanish moss and listen to the murmur of the waterfalls, you'll swear it was midnight in Dixie, not high noon in Anaheim. You can make reservations the day you plan to visit.

If you're looking for low-fat, more healthful food choices, consult your map. Restaurants that feature vegetarian choices are marked with a carrot. Numerous stands around the park offer fresh fruit, bottled juice, and even dill pickles!

Best Bets for Fast Food

Bengel Barbeque in Adventureland specializes in inexpensive chicken and beef on skewers. Unlike so much theme park food, this is spicy stuff. You can round out the meal with the fresh fruit plate or even that most elusive of all Disneyland foods—vegetables.

Disneyland offers its own version of a Happy Meal at most of the fast-food stands; for about $4 kids get either a hot dog, a burger, or chicken nuggets and fries, a drink, and a prize.

The Royal Street Veranda in New Orleans Square is small and the seating is very limited, but the food is tasty and unusual. You can get a "bowl" of clam chowder served in a scooped-out loaf of sourdough bread and a tasty fritter pastry, then carry your lunch to a nearby bench.

The Harbour Galley in Critter Country serves Cajun shrimp and scallops wrapped in bacon.

Daisy's Diner in Toontown is one of the only fast-food spots to offer pizza by the slice.

Hidden back in Big Thunder Ranch is the Big Thunder Barbeque, one of the best buys at Disneyland. In addition to kids' meals ($5), there's barbecue ribs and chicken, barbecue beef, and chicken sandwiches. This makes a good spot to take a break. There are plenty of family-style picnic tables topped with red-and-white-checked tablecloths.

You say a snack is all you need? Try the Mickey Mouse pretzels at the Brer Bar in Critter Country, a fritter from the Royal Street Veranda in New Orleans Square, a Really Big Cinnamon Roll from the Blue Ribbon Bakery on Main Street, or a Dole pineapple whip from the Tiki Juice Bar in Adventureland. Those in search of healthful snacks should head for the yogurt stands in Toontown and on Main Street or stop for fresh fruit and juice at one of the vendor carts.

PARADES, FIREWORKS, AND SHOWS

Although the attractions are thrilling, a trip to Disneyland wouldn't be complete without seeing a parade or show.

Parades

The current summer afternoon parade is based on the movie *Hercules*. The Hercules Victory Parade is kind of a watered-down parade, considering how great Disneyland parades can be, but the youngsters will enjoy it. During the busy season, the afternoon parade runs twice a day (usually at 2:30 and 4:30 P.M.) and twice on weekends during the off-season. Your map will note what is scheduled the day you visit. See "Tips for Watching the Parades" later in this section for more information.

As this book goes to press, the new evening parade scheduled for summer is called "Mulan," which is based on a new Disney animated feature. It is currently scheduled to run twice each evening.

During the Christmas season (defined as Thanksgiving through New Year's Day), Disneyland presents a special holiday parade. Although the parade is exciting, holiday crowds are up to four times as large as during the on-season. Locals pour through the gates—often just to take advantage of the special stuff—and it can be a crush. Also during this season, look for changes in It's a Small World. Its theme song changes to *Jingle Bells*, and the route is decorated in holiday themes from around the world.

The off-season parades are usually smaller, but as a rule they're offered daily.

Tips for Watching the Parades
 • Try to stake your curb space near the beginning point of the route. This can be trickier than it sounds. The parade runs from Main Street to Fantasyland and then is stored in Fantasyland until the next parade time, when it makes the return lap, heading back toward Main Street. Because the number of times a parade runs varies from day to day and season to season, there's no set way to predict which direction it'll be coming from. Ask one of the attendants putting up the ropes where the parade will originate. If it's starting from Fantasyland, find curb space there; if it's starting from Main Street, claim space as close as possible to the Town

Square hub. That way, after it passes you'll be able to move on to the less crowded rides while most of the people in the park are still watching the parade.

• The ideal spot for watching from Main Street is from the benches on the second level of the railroad station; it's an unobstructed view with comfortable seating, but you'll have to be there early to secure a bench. The curb, either on Main Street or in Fantasyland, is okay, and it's kind of a kick to be that close to the characters. The benches around the Matterhorn are more comfortable, but because you're pretty far back from the ropes, people may end up standing in front of you.

• During the busy season, arrive 30 minutes early for the afternoon parade and 45 minutes early for the evening parade. At less crowded times of the year, 15 minutes should suffice.

Fireworks

During the summer and holiday seasons, a rousing 15-minute fireworks display follows the first evening parade. Be sure not to miss Tinkerbell's Flight, a little-publicized but nifty extra. A young gymnast dressed as Tinkerbell slides by means of a suspended wire from the top of the Matterhorn over Sleeping Beauty Castle, a dazzling feat that leads directly into the fireworks. One of the best places to watch is probably the area around It's a Small World.

Even if you're not in the park at closing, you can view the fireworks from the Disneyland Hotel and many of the hotels along Harbor Boulevard. Be sure to ask whether you'll have a view of the park when you book your room.

Shows

Some of the special events listed below run only during the on-season, when Disneyland is open late. Before you visit, check with Guest Relations to confirm what will be running; you'll find daily show times noted on your entertainment schedule.

Fantasmic!—the laser-and-light extravaganza shown nightly at park closing time—is worth seeing at least once. A fountain-fireworks-and-laser show that features an emotional Armageddon-like battle between the good Disney characters and the evil ones, Fantasmic! plays over the Rivers of America at the park's closing time (twice on Saturdays). The show is a great favorite with kids 7 to 15, so be at the river at least 30 minutes before the scheduled show time to assure a good view. Some younger kids are frightened by the noise and bad guys, but because the show takes place outside, preschoolers can generally be distracted if the action becomes too intense.

Even if you decide against the show, you can benefit from its popularity. Because Fantasmic! draws huge crowds, the lines at major attractions suddenly shrink. If the lines at Splash Mountain have been prohibitive all day, try again about 15 minutes before Fantasmic! is scheduled to begin.

The Disneyland Hotel runs three types of shows: the character breakfasts (discussed earlier), the Neon Cactus (a family-style saloon show featuring singing, dancing, and two-step lessons), and Fantasy Waters (the free nightly music and fountain show by the lagoon). You don't have to be a guest at the hotel to take advantage of the shows.

The Golden Horseshoe Jamboree is a lively, and highly sanitized saloon show featuring Sam the bartender, the beauteous Miss Lilly, and lots of no-holds-barred singing and dancing. The lunch of burgers, hot dogs, fries, and cookies is filling, but be sure to make your reservations (in person) early.

Many smaller shows, some featuring the characters, appear around the park throughout the day. They vary from season to season, but your entertainment schedule will keep you up-to-date. Because so many bands perform around the park on a typical day, you may be able to combine even the most casual lunch with live music. Somehow it's these little-known extras that often wind up making the biggest impression. If you look up and see men in plaid shirts scaling the Matterhorn or doves circling Sleeping Beauty Castle at sunset, if you catch the strains of a Dixieland quartet in New Orleans Square, if your own son or daughter pulls the sword from the stone and is crowned ruler of all England, or if you and your spouse stash the kids on a bench and dance to a Cole Porter tune at the Carnation Plaza Garden, your vacation becomes more magical. Disneyland excels in creating these small moments, and perhaps we shouldn't be surprised that it's these things we remember long after the T-shirts are outgrown and the mouse ears are broken.

MEETING THE DISNEY CHARACTERS

Meeting the characters is a major objective for some families and a nice diversion for all. Many kids enjoy getting character autographs, and an autograph book can become a cherished souvenir upon your return home. If your children are very young, they might be overwhelmed by the characters, who are much larger in person than they appear on TV. Don't push it; the characters have been trained to be sensitive and will always wait for a child to approach them first. A kid who is nervous on the morning of the first day may be far more at ease by the evening of the second. You should prepare the kids for the fact that the characters whose faces are covered don't talk. As many as five young people in Mickey suits might be dispensed around Disneyland on a busy day, and they can't all be gifted with that familiar squeaky voice. So the characters communicate, pretty effectively, through body language. Also be aware that because of the construction of their costumes, the characters can't always see what's right beneath them. Donald and Daisy, for example, have a hard time looking over their bills, so they may ignore small children standing close by. If this seems to be the case, lift your child up to the character's eye level.

You can meet the characters at the Town Square hub of Main Street just after the park opens and in early afternoon, Toontown, the character breakfasts, and Critter Country (Pooh Stix Bridge).

AFTERNOON RESTING PLACES

Nothing is really as good as going back to your hotel room for a nap. But if you're short on time, you can rest up within the park at the following locations: Walt Disney Story and Great Moments with Mr. Lincoln, the railroad or monorail, the Disneyland Hotel for lunch, the Golden Horseshoe Jamboree, the Enchanted Tiki Room, the Country Bear Playhouse, the gazebo at the Carnation Plaza (where live entertainment plays every afternoon), and behind Miss Daisy's Boat in Toontown.

If your kids are wound up and restless but not tired enough to nap, try these locations, where a bit of running and yelping won't bother a soul: Tom Sawyer Island, Toontown, and the arcades and shooting galleries.

DISNEYLAND AFTER DARK

In addition to the special parades and shows, some attractions are especially dazzling by night. Head for these when the sun goes down: Splash Mountain, Big Thunder Mountain Railroad, Dumbo, King Arthur Carousel, Haunted Mansion, and It's a Small World.

BEST SOUVENIRS

• Autograph books, which can be purchased nearly anywhere on your first day in Disneyland. The signatures of the more obscure characters, like Eeyore or the Queen of Hearts, are especially to be valued.

• Miniature cars driven by Mickey, Minnie, or Donald for $5.

• Disney watches, with an outstanding selection at New Century Timepieces on Main Street. Check out the Goofy watch—it runs backward.

• Character Christmas ornaments, found at the Castle Christmas Shoppe in Fantasyland.

• Character cookie cutters or sandwich presses that stamp Mickey's visage onto toast and pancakes, available at Le Gourmet in New Orleans Square or at the Disneyland Hotel. A Disney-themed breakfast on your first Saturday home is a nice way to fight those post-trip blues.

• Kids who enjoyed Pirates of the Caribbean will want to stop at the nearby Pieces of Eight, where budding buccaneers can find hooks, hats, and eye patches. (You can even get a stuffed parrot to clip to your shoulder.) Children who prefer the Western theme of Frontierland will find an impressive selection of fake weaponry and cowboy clothes at the Westward Ho Trading Company.

• The Indiana Jones Adventure. If you survived the trip, you should buy a T-shirt to celebrate at the Indiana Jones Outpost.

• By far, the cheapest souvenirs are the prizes that come in the kiddie meals at the fast-food places. Some children start a collection of the Disney character pins—they look great stuck on a sailor cap!

• Antenna decorations are a great hit, and they're cheap. The Emporium sells out of them fast.

• And of course mouse ears have a sort of retro-chic. Get your name stitched on your pair at the Mad Hatter in Fantasyland.

BEST PLACES FOR FAMILY SNAPSHOTS

For those postcard-perfect scenes, Kodak has installed well-marked "photo spot" locations throughout the park. Two-hour photo development is available at Main Street Photo Supply on Main Street. If you really want to focus on your own kids, try the following locations:

• Riding Dumbo, just before takeoff. Once he rises, it's just too hard to get a good angle on the riders. (There's also a stationary Dumbo and a stationary teacup in Fantasyland, expressly for the purpose of posed shots.)

• In the flower-strewn market stall behind the portrait artists in New Orleans Square.

• On the movie set with Mickey in Toontown, which is the section of the park with the most unusual photo opportunities. Goofy's car is irresistible, or you could snap a shot of your child detonating the "bomb" outside the Fireworks Factory.

• A bit macabre, but fun: a group shot among the tombstones in front of the Haunted Mansion.

• With the characters, naturally. The best shots come from the character breakfasts, where you actually have time to pose. You might be able to snap a quick picture just by bumping into them on Main Street or in Toontown, but the odds are you'll get 36 unknown children from Michigan and somebody else's purse in the shot as well.

• A new development, seemingly adopted by most of the theme parks, is to have your mug snapped as you go careening down a scary point on a ride. Disneyland makes this possible at Splash Mountain. You can check out the photo first, then decide whether to purchase it. At Pooh Stix Bridge nearby, youngsters wait in line to pose with Eyeore, Tigger, or Pooh himself. A professional photographer takes these shots (like sitting on Santa's lap), and you purchase them at the end of the day at the photo shop on Main Street.

CAMCORDER TAPING TIPS

Camcorders can be heavy and bulky, and it's risky to leave them in strollers while you're inside attractions. If you decide to bring along the camcorder on only one day, make it the last day of your trip when you're revisiting favorite attractions—that way you'll leave with a Disneyland greatest-hits tape. If you need to stash your camcorder, there are lockers on Main Street or outside the main exit gate.

If you rent a camera or borrow one from someone back home, familiarize yourself with the machine before you actually begin to film. Novices tend to use rapid, jerky movements. When taping, don't pan or zoom too much because sudden camera movements disorient the viewer. If you're filming the kids on the teacups, for example, use the wide-angle lens and keep the camera stationary. Attempting to track them in close-ups as they spin past is too tough for anyone but a pro.

If you're using vocal commentary ("We're in Frontierland now, looking toward Big Thunder Mountain Railroad"), be sure to speak loudly. The background noise of the park will muffle your words.

Camcorder filming is allowed inside attractions, even those where flash photography is forbidden. Splash Mountain is the perfect attraction to film, but during the final plunge, there's a good chance the camera will get wet. Be sure your camcorder is safely zipped back into its case before the end of the ride.

Be sure to film special events (like the parades and character shows) and theater-style attractions (like the Country Bear Playhouse). The parades are especially fun to watch once you're home.

As you board the monorail, remember to ask whether the driver's cab is vacant. You may get the chance to ride up front, and one bonus is the chance to film panoramic views of the park.

CHAPTER 5

Disneyland:
Rides and Attractions

GETTING AROUND DISNEYLAND

Walking is by far the fastest means of transport in Disneyland. The vintage cars, horse-drawn carriages, and railroad are fun but not a very efficient way to get around the park. The monorail, which runs between Tomorrowland and the Disneyland Hotel, is another matter. You get a great overview of Disneyland and are in the middle of the park in no time. As a special treat, ask the attendant if you can ride up front with the driver. If you just want to ride the monorail for fun, you don't have to get off at the Disneyland Hotel. Sit tight, and you'll be on your way back to Tomorrowland within minutes.

SCARE FACTOR AT DISNEYLAND

Nothing at Disneyland is truly terrifying. In fact, young visitors raised on a steady diet of coasters called Corkscrew and Python are apt to find even Space Mountain pretty tame. But Disney plays on your emotions in more subtle ways. Teenagers who would seem to be anesthetized by the violence of movies like *Halloween VIII* have been known to sob inconsolably over the demise of *Old Yeller*. The attention to detail that is so much a Disney trademark is especially evident in attractions like the Indiana Jones Adventure—when that granite ball rolls toward you, it's believable. Because the emphasis is more on psychological than physical fear, it makes the scare factor tough to gauge. With the possible exception of Space Mountain and the Indiana Jones Adventure, nothing at Disneyland will knock off your glasses or shake out your fillings. But remember, Walt was the guy who bumped off Bambi's mother, and young children sometimes leave the rides shaken in a totally different way.

Keep in mind (where applicable) the height requirements included with the descriptions of the rides.

RIDES AND ATTRACTIONS IN DETAIL

The following should give you a good idea whether or not a ride is right for your child.

Main Street

Much of Main Street is devoted to restaurants, shops, information, and services. You can rent strollers and wheelchairs, buy film, cash a check, and mail a letter. Lost children are herded back to Main Street, and there's a fully supplied Baby Services Center and first-aid clinic there. You can pick up additional maps and entertainment schedules as well as check out which character breakfasts and dinner shows are running by stopping at Guest Relations.

Disneyland Railroad

Main Street is a good place to board the railroad, especially in the afternoon, when the other stations are swamped with people. The 20-minute ride takes you on a complete circle of the park, stopping in New Orleans Square, Toontown, and Tomorrowland. Trains run every six minutes. However, the train is not the fastest way to get from point A to point B; in the time you wait to board, you could've walked. Save the railroad for the afternoon, when you'll enjoy the chance to rest.

The Walt Disney Story and Great Moments with Mr. Lincoln

Older kids will benefit from learning a little more about the life of Walt Disney and can learn how the early cartoons were made. Almost everyone will be affected by the Audio-Animatronics figure of Abraham Lincoln, who rises from his chair and gives a brief talk composed of excerpts from speeches he wrote and delivered in his lifetime. The Lincoln robot moves subtly as the sky behind him changes from night to day. The inspirational message and the high-tech marvels will be lost on younger kids, but they may find this dark, quiet theater a good place to nap. Like most Main Street attractions, Great Moments with Mr. Lincoln is rarely crowded, and it's a good choice for the afternoon.

Main Street Cinema

Stop by the cinema and check out how Mickey has evolved through the years as six silent cartoons play simultaneously in this theater-in-the-round. The theater is small, requires you to stand, and isn't suited for long visits, but it's a good place for kids to kill a few minutes while parents shop.

Penny Arcade

If your children insist on stopping at an arcade, try to steer them toward this one with its quaint old machines, plaster fortune-tellers, massage-o-matic chairs, and hand-cranked movies. The name is no mere affectation either, as many of the machines take dimes, nickels, and even pennies, just like the machines of the good ol' days. This may be the most painless history lesson your kids ever receive.

Main Street Touring Tips

• Don't stop to savor the shops or minor attractions of Main Street in the morning—you need to hurry on to the big rides.

• Shop Main Street in the afternoon. Especially worthwhile are the Emporium and Disney Clothiers, which offer a staggering variety of character-themed toys and clothes. The Emporium, with its ink pens, wind-up toys, books, socks, and mugs, is a terrific source of stocking stuffers and party favors.

• Main Street is a good choice for lunch because the restaurants there are a little less crowded than those deep within the park. However, service at the sit-down restaurants can be very slow, so unless you're looking for a chance to rest, opt for a buffeteria or fast-food place.

• If you plan to watch one of the parades from Main Street, arrive at least 30 minutes before the parade starts to assure a good spot. Then, while some of you stretch out and hold the curb space, others can go for snacks, take a bathroom break, browse the shops, or visit the Penny Arcade.

• If you're not staying for the parade, be off Main Street 30 minutes before it's scheduled to begin. As time for the parade draws near, the street becomes so crowded you won't even be able to push a stroller on the sidewalk.

• After shopping, you can stow purchases at one of the lockers on Main Street or outside the exit turnstiles. If you're staying at the Disneyland or the Pacific Hotel, have packages sent back to your room. Just ask for Package Express when you pay for your purchase. The service is free.

Fantasyland

The aptly named Fantasyland, located directly behind Sleeping Beauty Castle, is a cross between a Bavarian village and a medieval fair. Most of the kiddie rides are here, and it's the most congested section of Disneyland.

Peter Pan's Flight

Tinkerbell flutters overhead as you board miniature pirate ships and sail above Nana's doghouse, the sparkling streets of London, the Indian camp, and Captain Hook's cove. Of all the Fantasyland rides, this one is most true to the movie that inspired it.

Mr. Toad's Wild Ride

Cars careen through a fun house, narrowly missing a chicken coop, an oncoming train, and a teetering grandfather clock. Because the cars are computer controlled, even a toddler can "drive," making this attraction a favorite with younger kids.

Snow White's Scary Adventures

Don't expect to leave this attraction humming *Whistle While You Work.* You ride mining cars through the dark, and the Wicked Witch appears several times quite suddenly. Although the ride isn't really terrifying, your toddler might find it scary. The acid test is this: How well did your kids handle the scene in the movie where Snow White is chased through the forest? My 14-year-old found this scary as a young child, and even now she thinks it's frightening. One 4-year-old claimed to like the ride while she was on it but, perhaps significantly, didn't want to try it again the next day. But the ride is a short one, and the special effects are fairly simple. *Final verdict:* Fine for most kids older than 4.

Pinocchio's Daring Journey

You travel with Pinocchio to Pleasure Island. The story sequence of this ride is a bit harder to follow than that of the other Fantasyland rides, and several parents reported that their kids were frightened by the characters and sudden noises. The music, however, is decidedly upbeat, and Pinocchio is safely at home with Geppetto in the final scene. The lines at Pinocchio never seem to be as long as those at nearby Peter Pan, Mr. Toad, or Snow White.

King Arthur Carousel
Seventy-two white horses prance while a pipe organ toots out *Chim-Chim-Cheree* and other classic Disney songs. This attraction is gorgeous at night.

Dumbo, the Flying Elephant
This happy little elephant has become the center of some controversy: Is he worth the wait or not? Although lines do move slowly, making a one-hour wait possible for a two-minute ride, there's something special about this attraction. It's frequently featured in the ads, so it's become an integral part of our collective Disney consciousness. Because riders make Dumbo fly by pushing a button, it's one of the few Fantasyland rides that isn't totally passive.

Mad Tea Party
These spinning pastel cups are propelled by their riders, and the speeds obtained range from breathtaking to giggle-making, so visitors of any age can enjoy the experience. Rider volume ebbs and flows at this attraction, which is slow to load, especially if only one attendant is on duty. If the lines look too daunting, check back later, as within a matter of minutes the crowd may have disappeared.

Casey Jr. Circus Train
Fans of the movie *Dumbo* will immediately recognize this attraction and queue up for the chance to circle Storybookland in animal cages. The cars are unbearably cramped for

adults, but the ride is so short and so tame that kids 3 and up can ride on their own.

Storybookland Canal Boats

A serene, scenic, and fairly lengthy ride, the canal boats circle Storybookland with its perfectly crafted miniatures from Disney movies. You'll drift past the home of Alice in Wonderland, Cinderella Castle, and the mine where the Seven Dwarfs worked. Young girls especially seem to delight in the miniatures, which are much like dollhouses rendered in exquisite detail. Like all the boat rides, this one is slow to load and best seen early in the morning or not at all. Because it follows basically the same path as the Casey Jr. Circus Train, families on a tight touring schedule might choose only one of the two. Just when you think the line is shortest, you discover that's because this ride closes during the parades.

Matterhorn

This venerable old ride is one of the few Fantasyland attractions not based on a beloved Disney movie. Although the ride looks a bit daunting as you stand on the ground gazing up, the Matterhorn is extremely popular with kids 5 to 8. Line up for the sheer thrill of the ride, which is basically one long zigzagging descent in and out of the mountain. Warn the kids to expect periodic blasts of Arctic air and more than one encounter with the Abominable Snowman.

The Matterhorn is a bit more intense (and higher) than Big Thunder Mountain Railroad. Your bobsled weaves in and out of the mountain, and riders experience the persistent sensation that it might, at any minute, leave the track and go hurling over the tents of Fantasyland. Glimpses of the Abominable Snowman and blasts of cold air support the illusion that you're on a runaway luge. The ride is a real kick, the kind you want to board over and over again. Riders must be at least 40 inches tall, and kids younger than 7 must ride with an adult. *Final verdict:* Fine for kids 7 and older. If your children between the ages 5 and 7 handled Splash Mountain and Big Thunder Mountain Railroad, they may be up for the Matterhorn.

Alice in Wonderland
You've got to love these caterpillar cars, and the ride inside is quite faithful to the story of Alice's drop down the rabbit hole. The special effects are entertaining enough to keep even adult riders amused.

Fantasyland Autopia
Open only when Tomorrowland Autopia is full or closed, this scaled-down version of the Tomorrowland Autopia allows kids to drive small race cars around a winding track. Although the cars are safe, be aware that some kids like to "crash" into each other. If you have a back or neck problem, you might want to stay away from this one. To drive alone, kids must be at least 52 inches tall and 7 years old. To drive with an adult, the minimum age is 1 year (but I wouldn't take toddlers on this ride).

It's a Small World
During this 11-minute boat ride, dolls representing children from every corner of the world greet you with a song so infectious you'll be humming it at bedtime. Although the lines look intimidating, they move fast. This is one of the best attractions to film with a camcorder.

Try to be nearby when the huge clock outside strikes the hour and the "children from all nations" emerge. If you can set it up, it's fun to be sailing out of the covered ride when the evening fireworks begin.

Sleeping Beauty Castle

The beautiful tile mosaics on the walls are worth stopping to see, and few visitors realize that you can actually enter the castle. The entrance is tucked away near the Tinkerbell Toy Shoppe, and a series of dioramas depicting the story of Sleeping Beauty await you inside. It takes about 10 minutes to walk through, and this is a tough attraction for families with toddlers. There are lots of steps, so little ones have to be carried, and the passageways are so tight that if your kid gets antsy or claustrophobic halfway through, it's nearly impossible to pass other visitors or backtrack to the entrance.

Fantasyland Touring Tips

• Visit Fantasyland before 11 A.M. or after 7 P.M.

• Don't eat or shop in Fantasyland. Similar food and toys can be found elsewhere in far less crowded areas of the park.

• Park your strollers in one spot and walk from ride to ride. Fantasyland is geographically small, so walking is easier than constantly loading and unloading the kids to push them only a few steps.

• Ride Dumbo first.

• Dumbo, Alice in Wonderland, King Arthur Carousel, Storybookland Canal Boats, and the Casey Jr. Circus Train can all have long lines, and all are exposed to the sun. Rather than letting the kids swelter, put one parent in line while the other takes the children for a drink or

potty break. As the queue makes its last turn before boarding, simply hand the kids over to the parent who has been
waiting in line.

Mickey's Toontown

Toontown, which opened in 1993, is a complete cartoon
community, so cleverly designed that the houses actually
resemble the characters who reside there. Toontown is
where Mickey and the gang work, play, and mingle with
their fans. Although adults enjoy seeing Goofy and Donald
and are amused by the innumerable in-jokes, Toontown is
really for young kids. Youngsters can talk to manholes, deto-
nate a bomb at the Fireworks Factory, bake a cake in Minnie's kitchen, or climb high into the woodsy tree house
where Chip 'n' Dale hang out.

Aside from the obvious advantage of getting the little
ones close to the characters, Toontown also breaks kids out
of that passive role of "ride riders" and lets them jump, run,
and play in a controlled environment. The characters begin
to show up in town square by midmorning; the Clocken-
spiel on City Hall alerts you to when the gang is on its way.
When the kids are antsy from a day of waiting in lines, a
few minutes in Goofy's Bounce House or Chip 'n' Dale's
Treehouse is a great way to burn off some excess energy.

Because Toontown is designed with safety in mind and
the attractions draw mostly kids under 10, parents can relax
on a bench or have dessert at Clarabelle's Frozen Yogurt and
just let the kids play. This is a good time to sneak a rest in a
cool spot behind Miss Daisy, Donald Duck's houseboat.

Roger Rabbit's Car Toon Spin

Roger Rabbit's Car Toon Spin, a combination of Mr. Toad's
Wild Ride and the Mad Tea Party, allows riders to actually

enter a cartoon. The little cars really hustle, and it's hard to predict when the bad-guy Weasels will spill the dip that sends the toons—and you—whirling in circles. You go through all the cartoon clichés, including the bull in a china shop, explosions, falling off a building, and seeing stars on impact. Although the montage of in-your-face animation and special effects is amusing, the actual ride is very tame and okay for even the youngest kids.

Roger Rabbit can draw lines of up to an hour in the afternoon. Either go midmorning or wait until evening.

Gadget's Go Coaster
A welcome addition for preschoolers who don't make the height requirements at the other coasters, Gadget's Go Coaster is one visual gag after another. Kids adore it, often clamoring to board again and again. It's a short ride— literally less than a minute long—but plenty zippy; it draws long lines in the afternoon.

Goofy's Bounce House
Kids flip over Goofy's Bounce House, where the inflated chairs are designed for climbing and leaping. An attendant lets in only a few kids at a time and makes sure play doesn't become dangerously rowdy.

Chip 'n' Dale's Treehouse and Acorn Crawl
Another great place to blow off steam, Chip 'n' Dale's Tree-house combines slides with a ball crawl. This makes a good photo "op."

Jolly Trolly
This wobbly little train, a spoof on those Beverly Hills tour buses that take visitors to the homes of the stars, runs from

Roger Rabbit's Car Toon Spin to Mickey's House. It's one of the cleverest sight-gags in Toontown.

Mickey's House

The highlight of Toontown is Mickey's red-shingled, curvy-sided house with his private movie studio in the back. After touring the house, you'll get to meet Mickey "on the set" of either *Steamboat Willie, Through the Mirror, The Sorcerer's Apprentice,* or *The Band Concert.*

Tip: Disney jealously guards Mickey's star status, having him appear around the park less frequently and for shorter periods of time than the other characters. Because TV ads give the impression that Mickey is everywhere, practically serving up popcorn and driving the monorail, some kids become upset when they've spent an entire day at Disneyland without seeing the Main Mouse. Toontown neatly solves that problem, as everyone who queues up at Mickey's house will have time for pictures and autographs. And because visitors are admitted into the studio in controlled numbers, toddlers and preschoolers are never trampled by older kids.

Minnie's House

Minnie's house is a marvel of automation. In her dressing room, young girls can sample a whiff of her Eau de Bubble Gum perfume, the dishwasher and oven in the kitchen actually "work," and her answering machine is full of messages from Mickey.

Donald's Houseboat

Miss Daisy, Donald Duck's houseboat, is docked in Toon Lake and is scaled and colored to look like Donald himself. A fun climb-and-crawl space for young kids.

Toontown Touring Tips

• If your children are young and will want to spend a lot of time in Toontown, go there in the morning, immediately after you visit the major attractions of Fantasyland. Ride Gadget's Go Coaster and Roger Rabbit's Car Toon Spin first. Then leave for another area of the park.

• Return to Toontown around lunchtime (you'll find pizza and frozen yogurt here) or in the early afternoon, when the characters come out in full force. This is also a good time to let younger kids play in Goofy's Bounce House or Chip 'n' Dale's Treehouse or among the interactive exhibits near the Gag Factory, but steer clear of the rides.

• If you miss the chance to ride Gadget's Go Coaster or Roger Rabbit's Car Toon Spin in the morning, wait until evening to try them. Toontown clears out in the evening when the kiddies head home.

• With its funky visual gags, Toontown is a great place to take pictures. Pose the kids in Goofy's creatively parked car, detonating a bomb, or boarding the Jolly Trolly.

Tomorrowland

If you haven't been back to Disneyland since the Flying Saucers (1960s) or even in the past year, you're in for a surprise. Tomorrowland was rapidly becoming "Yesterdayland" in this world of high technology and space exploration, so Disney decided to totally update and renovate. But don't worry: Favorites like Star Tours and Space Mountain were saved and improved for all the preteens, teens—and adults—who can't wait to get in line. While keeping these popular rides, Disneyland has added some more. As this book goes to press, the following rides haven't opened yet. From their descriptions, however, they're sure to be instant hits.

Tomorrowland: New Attractions

Astro Orbitor

Nascent astronauts get the chance to pilot a spaceship through a universe of mysterious planets and constellations—animated, of course. The height restriction hasn't been determined yet nor are we sure of age-appropriateness.

Rocket Rods

This one is sure to have a height—and probably an age—requirement. Five-passenger vehicles surpass the speed of some roller coasters, traveling over, around, and through Tomorrowland and following the path of the "old" People-Mover.

Honey, I Shrunk the Audience

Taking the place of Captain EO, this show is a combination of 3-D systems and other special effects, including a moving floor. If you've been to Epcot, you'll be familiar with a version of this. The show is purported to be funny and fun, with the audience being "shrunk" by one of the off-beat inventions. This one will be a great family show for all ages.

Innoventions

When Tomorrowland opened in the 1950s, it boasted the House of the Future—a house and its furnishings made entirely of plastic. Then the same spot was occupied by the America Sings show. Now it's home to Innoventions, where the technology of the future is presented in a two-level interactive pavilion. The world's leading industries show their future wares in five technology sections, and you get to touch and operate many of them.

Tomorrowland: "Old" Familiar Attractions

Space Mountain

This three-minute coaster ride through inky darkness is the major scream-ripper in Disneyland. The cars neither move very fast nor go very high, at least not in comparison to monster coasters at other theme parks, but the special effects lift Space Mountain far above the ordinary. The new renovations have added state-of-the-art equipment, so riders get their own sound system of synchronized music, narration, and sound effects, all timed to work with the corresponding locations on the ride.

Children younger than 7 must have an adult present to ride. Pregnant women and children younger than 3 or less than 40 inches tall are prohibited. Some kids ages 3 to 7 love Space Mountain, but some I surveyed found it too scary. Kids ages 7 to 11 gave the ride a solid thumbs-up.

Tip: With all the coasters, Disney employees are happy to help families with young children break up their party so that everyone except the baby gets to ride. Just tell the attendant that you'll need to do a "baby swap." This does not mean that you can trade in your howling toddler for that angelically napping infant behind you—only that one parent can ride first while the other waits with the baby. Then the attendant hands the baby over to the parent who is disembarking, and the waiting parent gets to ride. If it isn't too busy, older children may be allowed to ride twice: once with Mom and once with Dad.

It's the fact that the whole ride takes place inside, in utter darkness, that makes Space Mountain unique. There are plenty of dips and turns, and you can't see them in order to brace yourself. The intensity is also sustained; unlike Splash Mountain, where the scary part is over in three seconds flat, Space Mountain keeps you screaming from start to finish. This is not a good choice for anyone prone to motion sickness, regardless of age. *Final verdict:* Forget it for preschoolers. Kids 5 to 9 are iffy, but kids 9 and older loved the ride.

Star Tours
Motion-simulation technology and a joggling cabin combine to produce the real feel of flight in Star Tours. With the hapless Captain Rex at the helm, your crew is off for what is promised to be a routine mission to the Moon of Endor. But if you think the mission is going to be routine, you don't know diddly about Disney. "Don't worry if this is your first flight," Rex comforts visitors as they board, "it's my first one, too." One wrong turn later, and you're ripping through the fabric of space at hyperspeed, headed toward combat with the dreaded Death Star. George Lucas served as creative consultant, and the ride features the charming as well as the scary elements of his Star Wars series. The chatter of R2D2, C3PO, and assorted droids makes even the queues enjoyable. Star Tours is the best of both worlds, with visual effects so convincing that you'll clutch your arm rails, but the actual rumbles are so mild that only the youngest children are eliminated as potential crew members. The height requirement is 40 inches.

Although your seat is actually moving very little, you'll pitch from side to side a bit. But with angles no greater than you'd get in a malfunctioning recliner, it really feels as if you're flying. A few parents reported that their kids threw up (for that matter, so did a couple of parents), but the effects of the motion-simulation technology can be lessened by simply looking away from the screen. Most kids surveyed loved this ride, especially if they had seen the Star Wars movies. *Final verdict:* Fine for kids 5 and older, as long as they're not prone to motion sickness.

Submarine Voyage

The submarine ride features sunken treasure, octopi, and other (fake) marine life, culminating in an attack by a giant squid. There's a real split of opinion here. Some families rated this ride highly, whereas others said that the loading was slow, the wait long, and the ride pedestrian. If you want to try it for yourself and form your own judgment, go before 11 A.M. or after 8 P.M.

Starcade

Consider this an arcade on steroids, a multilevel extravaganza with over 250 games, some of which will undoubtedly be new even to the most ardent arcadeophile. One word of warning: It is impossible to send the kids in here "for a couple of minutes." If you're not prepared to wander around for an hour, don't enter these blinking doorways at all.

Tomorrowland Autopia

Tiny sports cars, which any child over 52 inches can drive, lap a nifty-looking racetrack. Car-crazed kids 4 to 11 enjoy the ride, but adults and older kids are likely to find the cars too slow for their taste.

Tip: Children who don't make the height requirement can still steer the cars as long as Mom or Dad is there to give it the gas.

Tomorrowland Touring Tips

• Families planning to ride Space Mountain should be there before 10 A.M. If you have more than one day at Disneyland, start out in Tomorrowland on your second day and ride Space Mountain and Star Tours first.

• If you don't plan to ride Space Mountain or Star Tours, save Tomorrowland for afternoon. Remember that new rides, like Rocket Rods and Astro Orbitor, will be popular, too. Honey, I Shrunk the Audience will also draw crowds, but at least it's in a high-capacity venue.

• If you're looking for fast food during peak dining times, the Tomorrowland food stands are never as busy as those in other sections of the park. The Tomorrowland Terrace is especially snappy, with the added bonus of live music in the afternoon.

Adventureland

Thematically the most bizarre of all the lands, sort of a "Bourbon Street meets Trinidad by way of the Congo," Adventureland manages to convey an exotic mood.

Indiana Jones Adventure

This is still the hottest and by far the most thrilling ride in Disneyland. The Indiana Jones Adventure is neither a coaster nor a motion-simulated film. Guests actually enter the Temple of the Forbidden Eye for an action-packed ride in a 12-person Jeep. You'll encounter everything Indy does in the popular film series, climaxing when the infamous granite ball comes rolling right toward your Jeep.

The excitement begins building in the queue area (which is fortunate because there can be a two-hour wait on a busy day). The chambers are ornate and atmospheric, and by the time you board the ride you're definitely in the mood for adventure. The temple holds three types of treasure: unlimited wealth, eternal youth, and the ability to see into the future. Depending on what the people in your Jeep "choose," you'll start off on one of three different paths, with myriad programmed cues assuring that each Jeepload of guests experiences a slightly different variation of the ride.

As you roll toward the temple deity Mara, you're repeatedly warned not to look into her forbidden eye, or you will be pronounced unworthy and have to face the wrath of the goddess. Well, big shock—everybody looks, everybody's unworthy, and everybody has to face the wrath of Mara, which comes in the form of explosions, poison darts, snakes, bats, and collapsing suspension bridges. The Audio-Animatronic Harrison Ford figure, which pops up several times to advise or berate you, is the most lifelike figure Disney has ever created.

Between the wild movements of the Jeeps, which careen, plunge, and bump through the movie set, and the exciting special effects, which scarcely give you time to recover from one before the next is on you, you'll encounter a new experience every 18 seconds. The 46-inch height requirement is due partly to the intensity of the ride but mostly to the construction of the Jeeps. Shorter children simply wouldn't be able to see anything. However, there is no age restriction.

Come first thing in the morning—especially if you're let in an hour early through the Flex Passport or Magic Morning perk (see Disneyland Hotel in Chapter 2) or prepare for a wait of between 90 minutes and 2 hours. Check the information center near the Carnation Plaza for wait times. Despite the inconvenience, the ride is worth the wait.

The height requirement automatically eliminates most kids younger than 7. There's a lot of jostling and bouncing during the ride, and the special effects (you actually feel the wind from the poison darts blowing across the top of your head) are utterly convincing. But kids 7 to 11 who were surveyed loved this ride, especially if they had seen the movie and knew what to expect. If you think your kids might be a little iffy, be sure they don't sit on the sides where they're closer to the snakes and other "critters." *Final verdict:* If you're tall enough to ride, then ride.

Jungle Cruise

You'll meet up with headhunters, hyenas, water-spewing elephants, and other varieties of frankly fake wildlife on this 15-minute boat ride. The jokey patter of your tour guide helps the trip along, and the cruise is a hit with younger kids. Try it in the evening, when the special effects are more believable. The guides keep things light with their running patter, and the elephants, rhinos, headhunters, and snakes are played for laughs. *Final verdict:* Fine for anyone, especially if you go during daylight.

Swiss Family Robinson Treehouse

A real split of opinion here: Some visitors love this replica of the ultimate tree house, whereas others rate it as dull. But there's rarely much of a wait, and certain aspects of the tree house, such as the plumbing, are incredibly clever. Some of the pieces furnishing the tree house are from the 1960s movie. One word of warning: This is a tough attraction to tour with toddlers. There are many steps, and at times the climbing is too precarious for unsteady little legs. Lugging a 2-year-old up and down is tiring, but the real problem is that the bamboo and rigging look so enticing that kids want to climb on their own and at their own pace. This may not sit well with the 200 people in line behind you.

Enchanted Tiki Room

Interestingly, these singing/talking birds and the singing/talking flowers and totem poles around them represent Disney's first attempt at the Audio-Animatronics that are now such an integral part of attractions like Pirates of the Caribbean. As with the tree house, this attraction draws a large range of ratings, from "cute" to "hokey," but the Tiki Birds strut their stuff in a cool, quiet theater, making this a good choice for the afternoon. Very young children love to sing along with the colorful birds. The 3-year-old interviewed loved the show and was not scared at all of the sudden thunder and lightning. There's even a restroom hidden here.

New Orleans Square

Lovely, shady, and by far the best place in the park for a meal, New Orleans Square is also home to two major attractions.

Pirates of the Caribbean

Pirates of the Caribbean inspires great loyalty, and a significant number of guests named this oldie-but-goodie their favorite attraction at Disneyland. Your boat goes over two small waterfalls, and the swirling mists and the splash of cannonballs add to the atmosphere. But it's the Audio-Animatronics buccaneers that make the ride so terrific—they're menacing, humorous, and whimsical. A few kids become frightened, but most agree with the 5-year-old who voted the ride "the best reason to leave Fantasyland."

The drafty, dungeon-like queue area gives you a glimpse of what the ride will be like. Although there are gunshots, skeletons, cannons, mangy-looking buccaneers, and even a couple of drops over "waterfalls" in the dark, the mood is up-tempo and the music peppy. *Final verdict:* Fine for kids 5 and older. There is no height requirement for this ride.

Haunted Mansion

More apt to elicit a giggle than a scream, the Haunted Mansion is full of clever special effects. The cast members, who dress as morticians, contribute considerably to the fun with such instructions as "Drag your wretched bodies to the dead center of the room." After a trip down—or is it up?—in the infamous stretching room, you're loaded into black "doom buggies" for a ride through the 999 "happy haunts" that live in the mansion. The mansion is home to ravens, floating objects, swirling ghosts, glowing crystal balls, and doors that rap when no one's there. If you have the courage, the Haunted Mansion can be especially fun at night.

More funny than scary. *Final verdict:* Fine for kids 7 and older. Kids 5 to 7 will be okay, unless they're afraid of the dark.

Disney Gallery

Adults, older kids, and anyone interested in animation should climb the steps above the Pirates of the Caribbean and take a look at the displayed "cels" from classic Disney movies. This is not a good stop for those with young kids in tow, however—this is original art, and it's pricey.

Adventureland and New Orleans Square Touring Tips

• Because of the popularity of Indiana Jones, the streets of Adventureland are mobbed all day long. See the attractions, but save shopping and eating for less crowded sections of the park.

• New Orleans Square, in contrast, is a great place for lunch. Some of the most appealing—and pricey—restaurants in Disneyland are located here.

• If you miss a major attraction in the morning, try visiting it during the afternoon parade, when the crowds taper off somewhat.

Frontierland

Kids love the rough-and-tumble Wild West feel of Frontierland, which is home to several of Disneyland's most time-honored attractions.

Big Thunder Mountain Railroad

A roller coaster disguised as a runaway mine train, Big Thunder is less scary than Space Mountain but almost as popular. It's an exciting, well-loved three-minute ride. The glory of the ride is in the setting: You zoom through a deserted mining town filled with bats and falling rocks. If you're wondering whether the coaster may be too much for your kids, be advised that Big Thunder is more in the rattle-back-and-forth than the lose-your-stomach-as-you-plunge tradition. Our teenage friends noted that if you like coasters, try for the end car. Children younger than 7 must ride with an adult, and the 40-inch height requirement does apply. Almost any child older than 7 should be able to handle the dips and twists; preschoolers are iffier, but any kid who liked the Matterhorn and Splash Mountain is apt to love Big Thunder as well. But consider skipping this one if you have any neck problems.

The train goes fast but not high, and riders exit giggly but not shaky. *Final verdict:* Fine for kids 5 and older.

Golden Horseshoe Jamboree
Hot dogs, burgers, fries, and cookies are served during this 30-minute saloon show, which is full of hokey humor and lively dancing. Young kids won't get all the jokes, but the humor is delivered in such broad style that they may find themselves laughing even when they're not sure why. Between making reservations, eating, and the show, you'll invest a good 90 minutes, so visit this show only if you're going to be in Disneyland two days or longer. Folks line up early for this one—even with reservations. Reservations can be made only in person.

Frontierland Shootin' Arcade
Bring quarters. This is a pretty standard shooting gallery— fun for the kids in the afternoon.

Mark Twain Steamboat
The second tier of this paddle-wheel riverboat offers great views of the Rivers of America. But as with the other watercraft, board only if you have time to kill and the boat is at the dock. There are a few seats, but most riders stand.

Sailing Ship Columbia
A lovely replica of the first American ship to circumnavigate the globe, the Columbia is highly detailed and a pleasure to board. But it's added to the fleet only during busy seasons.

Mike Fink Keelboats
As opposed to the Columbia and the Mark Twain, only a few people at a time load these small keelboats, so if you're on a tight touring schedule, opt for one of the larger boats. Although the exposed top decks offer the best views, sitting

up there in the afternoon sun can be sweltering. This attraction is open only in summer.

Tom Sawyer Island

A getaway playground full of caves, bridges, forts, and windmills, Tom Sawyer Island is a good destination when the kids become too rambunctious to handle. The one drawback is that the island is accessible only by raft, which means you often have to wait to get there and then wait to get back. If your kids are younger than 5, don't bother making the trip. The terrain is too rough and widespread for preschoolers to play without constant adult supervision. But if your kids are 5 and older and beginning to go wild, stop off at Tom Sawyer Island, where such behavior is not only acceptable but *de rigueur*. The island closes at dusk.

Fantasmic!

See Chapter 4 for a description of this show.

Critter Country

This small, charming land, composed primarily of Splash Mountain and the Country Bear Playhouse, is tucked away from the hubbub of Frontierland and New Orleans Square. There are small benches, carved to resemble critters, where you can rest in the shade unperturbed—except for the occasional shrieks coming from the direction of Splash Mountain. Or put your feet up at the Hungry Bear Restaurant, which offers counter service and glorious treetop views of the Rivers of America.

Splash Mountain

Splash Mountain, a hybrid thrill ride and theme ride, is based on the movie *Song of the South*. It takes riders on a watery, winding journey as Brer Bear and Brer Fox pursue Brer Rabbit through swamps and bayous. There's a big buildup to the culmination—a 40-mile-an-hour drop over a five-story waterfall. *Zip-a-Dee-Doo-Dah,* perhaps the most hummable of all Disney theme songs, fills the air, making the ride both charming and exhilarating. Your picture is snapped during the plunge, and you can purchase it near the exit. The strategy that works so well in Fantasyland— putting one person in line and joining them later—is impossible at Splash Mountain, where the queue area has innumerable twists and turns. Stick together; if you leave the kids in line and go for a refreshment, they might be hard to spot when you return. The line is longer than it looks at first. You will definitely get wet in the front or back seats. Naturally, there is a convenient gift store near the exit where you can purchase dry T-shirts. This could be the time you get the kids that sweatshirt you promised.

The atmosphere is happy and kid oriented, but the last drop is so steep that you have the feeling you're coming out of your seat. Splash Mountain was rated highly among kids 5 to 7 who made the height cut; if you have doubts, stand in front of the waterfall and let your kids watch a few logs take that final plunge before they decide. The anticipation for that last plunge is uppermost in most people's minds, so they don't even notice the mother rabbit crying because her baby rabbit was going to be fed to the fox. Kids must be at least 3 years old and over 40 inches tall to ride. *Final verdict:* Fine for kids 5 and older.

Country Bear Playhouse

Kids love the funny, furry, Audio-Animatronics bears featured in this 15-minute show. From the coy Teddi Beara to the incomparable Big Al, each face is distinctive and lovable.

Although the Playhouse is extremely popular, it is able to seat large crowds at once. Try it in the afternoon.

Davy Crockett Explorer Canoes

These canoes are human powered, which makes them appealing to some and appalling to others. Your guide, decked out in a coonskin cap and buckskins, steers the boat while the novices paddle along. Kids 7 to 11 love the chance to row, and there's no height requirement, although kids under 6 must wear life jackets. This attraction closes at dusk.

Pooh Stix Bridge

You can't miss the parents and youngsters lined up here, next to the gift shop, for a chance to have their pictures taken with Pooh or Eyeore. It's just like taking a picture with Santa Claus. Be prepared to wait 45 minutes (about 20 minutes off-season) for meeting with your favorite character. Autographs and pictures are usually given from 11 A.M. to 6 P.M. A photographer snaps the photo, which you can then purchase for $10 to $15 at the Kodak photo shop on Main Street.

Frontierland and Critter Country Touring Tips

• If you're looking to rest up on a crowded and hot summer afternoon, try the Country Bear Playhouse or the Golden Horseshoe Jamboree, where you can sit and be entertained in air-conditioned comfort.

• Two Frontierland attractions close at dusk: Tom Sawyer Island and all the Rivers of America watercraft.

• If you learn the location of only one attraction prior to your arrival at Disneyland, make it Splash Mountain. It is essential that you get to Splash Mountain early to avoid long lines, but it is deep within Critter Country and hard to find by just wandering around. Get a map and plot your path through Adventureland and New Orleans Square so that you don't get lost on your dash to the Splash. Check the information kiosk to see how long the wait will be, and then decide whether to try it then or during a parade. The opening of the new Tomorrowland attractions might pull away some of the usual crowds.

BEST ATTRACTIONS FOR KIDS

Here's a breakdown of the best rides for each age group.

Don't-Miss List for Kids 3 to 7
Admittedly, age 7 is an arbitrary cutoff point. If your 6-year-old likes wilder rides, consult the list for kids 7 to 11.

    Splash Mountain (if they pass the height
       requirement)
    Pirates of the Caribbean
    Country Bear Playhouse
    Toontown (anything)
    It's a Small World
    Dumbo
    Peter Pan's Flight
    Mad Tea Party
    Alice in Wonderland
    Honey, I Shrunk the Audience
    The parades
    The character breakfasts
    The character autographs

Worth-Your-While List for Kids 3 to 7
Jungle Cruise
Swiss Family Robinson Treehouse
Haunted Mansion (for kids 5 and older)
Tom Sawyer Island
Snow White's Scary Adventures
Pinocchio's Daring Journey
Mr. Toad's Wild Ride
King Arthur Carousel
Submarine Voyage
Storybookland Canal Boats
Big Thunder Mountain Railroad (for kids 5 and
    older)
Fantasmic!

Don't-Miss List for Kids 7 to 11
Almost everything is appropriate for children this age, who
are apt to enjoy both the coasters and the character-themed
rides.
Indiana Jones Adventure
Splash Mountain
Matterhorn
Space Mountain
Big Thunder Mountain Railroad
Star Tours
Pirates of the Caribbean
Country Bear Playhouse
It's a Small World
Mad Tea Party
Haunted Mansion
Honey, I Shrunk the Audience
Fantasmic!
The parades

Worth-Your-While List for Kids 7 to 11
   Jungle Cruise
   Swiss Family Robinson Treehouse
   Toontown
   Tom Sawyer Island
   Mr. Toad's Wild Ride
   Peter Pan's Flight
   Tomorrowland Autopia
   Davy Crockett Explorer Canoes

Don't-Miss List for Preteens and Teens
Children over the age of 11 will have these rides at the top
of their must-ride list.
   Indiana Jones Adventure
   Star Tours
   Space Mountain
   Splash Mountain
   Matterhorn
   Big Thunder Mountain Railroad
   Pirates of the Caribbean
   Haunted Mansion
   Fantasmic!
   Tomorrowland Autopia
   New Tomorrowland rides
   The parades

Worth-Your-While List for Preteens and Teens
   Davy Crockett Explorer Canoes
   Starcade
   Roger Rabbit's Car Toon Spin
   Some of the character-themed rides in Fantasyland are
      so uncool that they're cool. Teenagers seem to like
      Mr. Toad's Wild Ride and the Mad Tea Party best.

CHAPTER *6*

Life After Disneyland

KNOTT'S BERRY FARM

As Southern California is known for fantasy, artifice, and hype, it might surprise you to learn that Knott's Berry Farm really did begin as a berry farm and, until very recently, was run by the Knott family. When her husband Walter's boysenberry business turned sour during the Depression, Cordelia Knott opened a small restaurant featuring fried chicken and boysenberry pie. Cordelia's culinary skills were well known locally, and the restaurant soon became such a roaring success that Walter Knott began to devise simple pony rides and other Old West–themed amusements to entertain the people waiting in line. From these humble and accidental beginnings sprang the oldest theme park in the nation. It still revolves around a California gold rush theme and still serves knockout fried chicken and boysenberry pie. Recently, it was announced that the park would be sold but that nothing would change. There are plans to add a giant wooden roller coaster. Currently, the park consists of six themed areas beyond the gates, a marketplace that does not have an entry fee, and the famous Mrs. Knott's Chicken Dinner Restaurant.

Details

8039 Beach Boulevard, Buena Park
714-827-1776 or 714-220-5200

Located in Buena Park, about 15 minutes from Disneyland, Knott's can be toured in a day. Tickets are $32 for adults, $24 for kids 3 to 11; but off-season specials often drop the rates, and it's easy to find discount coupons as well. During the summer, when the park stays open late, adults can enter after 4 P.M. for $16 and kids for $12. Parking will cost you an extra $6 no matter what time you arrive. Because Knott's is a relatively small park, it's quite possible to see the major attractions in four to five hours, so late entry isn't a bad option.

Many Anaheim hotels run shuttles to Knott's Berry Farm, or it is easy to get there by car. However, once you've exited the freeway, you'll have to look hard for the signs leading you to the park. When you leave at night, there are few directions leading you back to the freeway and no one in the parking lot to help. It's best to get that information from one of the Knott's personnel before you leave. You can request maps in advance by calling 714-220-5200. Summer hours are 9 A.M. to midnight; the rest of the year, the park is open from 10 A.M. to 6 P.M. weekdays, with longer hours on weekends.

Strollers and wheelchairs can be rented; there are lockers in Ghost Town and near Big Foot Rapids (where you can stash the dry clothes you'll need after the water ride!).

Highlights

The beauty of Knott's is the fact not only that you can tour it in one day but also that it's more than an amusement park. It's not the place for glitzy displays and daredevil rides, although the kids do like the rides and the arcades. There are surprises around many corners in Ghost Town, for instance, because the designers used the history of the West to its advantage. Lifelike recreations of a Western-style barber shop, Gold Rush–era laundry, and a "typical" jail are found on the streets. A working blacksmith and a replicated gold mine and working sluice where the kids can pan for gold (for an extra charge beyond admission) enable the kids to ask questions. Explain to the kids that some of the buildings they're seeing are authentic and were actually moved to this site from various towns in California and Arizona.

Ghost Town is also where you'll find the Wild West Stunt Show, which I found to be a major disappointment but the kids thought was funny. It's long on stupid jokes and short on stunts. The sudden sound of the cap gun scared the daylights out of a couple of toddlers. Warn youngsters in advance of what's to come. Arrive early to grab a seat in the shade. There's also a parody of old-fashioned entertainment at the Calico Saloon.

Nearby Indian Trails is more of a participatory area, and it's a good place to take elementary school–aged kids and preschoolers. Children can explore a Native American tepee, for instance, and usually there's someone demonstrating beading or painting. The kids can participate, and there's a charge for supplies. Mexican Indians demonstrate the dances and musical instruments once used by the Aztecs in Mexico. When the show is over, stop for Native American fry bread at the nearby food stand.

Preschoolers are bound to enjoy Camp Snoopy, where they'll find lots of kiddie rides, climbing forts, play areas, and the Peanuts characters. The Petting Zoo is home to some really bold goats (who butt you into feeding them) and a down-home merry-go-round pulled by a mule. There's a quick, mild roller coaster that even hesitant youngsters seem willing to try. One of our very favorite attractions in Camp Snoopy is Beary Tales, a tree house where children can explore and climb. Although most children report that this attraction is great fun, there are some dark, semi-enclosed "trails" along the way that may prove to be too claustrophobic for your child. Be prepared to escort him out. The shows in Camp Snoopy are especially geared toward youngsters. Be sure to stick around for the animal shows presented in the outdoor Camp Snoopy Theater. Kids can even touch and pet tame raccoons, wolves, and other forest creatures.

Next door to Camp Snoopy are Fiesta Village and the Roaring '20s, which are full of attractions that appeal to kids 7 to 11. This is where the popular Montezooma's Revenge and Jaguar! roller coasters can be found as well as shake-'em-up rides such as Tampico Tumbler and Mexican Hat Dance (more about these later). The nineteenth-century carousel is considered one of America's finest.

Boardwalk, depicting the quintessential Southern California beach lifestyle, is *the* area for the teenagers in your group. XK-1, Boomerang, Windjammer, Log Ride, and Sky Jump are rides that will keep them busy. Boardwalk is also home to Hammerhead (which we even had trouble watching, it was so nauseating), Kingdom of the Dinosaurs, Goodtime Theater, and the bumper cars. Airheadz, an arcade/food court/music center, is probably the best place to find "missing" teens.

The sixth themed area is Wild Water Wilderness, home to Bigfoot Rapids, a great ride for the family, and the new Mystery Lodge, a beautiful multisensory and special effects show that is a tribute to Native American culture. When campfire smoke begins to illustrate the storyteller's words, the children are mesmerized. Because shows run every half hour all day, Mystery Lodge is a good choice for the afternoon and is appropriate for all ages.

Rides

Knott's Berry Farm has three levels of rides: the coasters and spinning rides (Hammerhead, Windjammer, Jaguar!, Montezooma's Revenge, and Boomerang), the medium-intensity rides (Parachute Sky Jump, Headache, Bumper Cars, and others), and the kiddie rides found in Camp Snoopy. The water rides and shows are appropriate for any age-group.

It's hard to say which of the coasters was the most popular, because the kids surveyed rode each one more than once and really liked them. Eleven-, 12-, and 13-year-olds rushed off Montezooma's Revenge, then rushed right back on two and three more times. The three 11-year-olds interviewed loved Boomerang the best and rode it three times. Windjammer, a dual-track steel coaster, got rave reviews from my 14-year-olds. Jaguar!, a roller coaster built around a Mayan pyramid, swerves, banks, and twists, simulating a cat stalking its prey. This huge beast covers over one-sixth of the park's total area, at one point actually passing through the 360-degree loop of Montezooma's Revenge. Jaguar! is exciting and visually impressive (especially at night) but actually tamer than the other coasters at Knott's. Kids older than 7 should be able to handle it, assuming they pass the 42-inch height requirement.

XK-1 could definitely make someone sick. In fact, pregnant women aren't allowed to ride it. At 70 feet up, you're allowed to take control of your own car. Turning it upside down seems to be the point. Hammerhead (48-inch height requirement) looks awful. I couldn't even stay around to talk to anyone about it. Lest I sound squeamish, two other adults, whose spouses were on board, couldn't watch it either!

Scare Factor

Of the three coasters, Jaguar! is best suited for younger kids, assuming they pass the 42-inch height requirement. Montezooma's Revenge is more intense than Jaguar!, and Boomerang and Windjammer are the wildest coasters in the park. Preschoolers not up to a coaster will enjoy Twister in Camp Snoopy or the Soap Box Racers.

Parachute Sky Jump is no place for anyone with a fear of heights, but the landing is quite gentle, and the ride was a great favorite among kids surveyed.

Neither of the water rides is terribly intense, although that last drop on the Log Ride might eliminate some preschoolers as potential riders. Bigfoot Rapids makes only small descents, and because the entire family can ride together, this white-water adventure is fine for most kids (there's a 36-inch height requirement). We rode it with a 3-year-old who loved it. You will get wet—possibly soaked—in the summer when the waterfalls are turned on; if it's a chilly day or your child might be unnerved by the splashing, skip Bigfoot Rapids.

Kingdom of the Dinosaurs brings you up close and personal with large-scale robotic dinosaurs, but most kids are such dinosaur junkies that they love the ride. It's dark inside, and there's a great deal of prehistoric roaring, but the ride is designed to be more atmospheric than terrifying and is fine for all ages. However, if your child scares easily, stay away from these giant monsters.

Although Montezooma's Revenge, Jaguar!, Boomerang, and Windjammer get credit for being the "biggies" at Knott's, Tampico Tumbler and XK-1 will appeal to some of your kids. But skip these if you're prone to motion sickness. Boomerang stops with a big jerk; when some children exited Windjammer, we heard complaints about their heads hitting the sides of the seats. First you do the whole ride facing the front, then the whole ride again going backward.

Just because Tampico Tumbler and Mexican Hat Dance are relatively close to Camp Snoopy, don't automatically assume they're right for preschoolers. Watch a go-around before you commit.

Calico Mine Ride takes kids alone if they're 6 years or older, and it goes through a dark, replicated mine. If your youngsters have any fear of the dark, be sure to warn them of what will happen.

Touring Tips

• Hang on to the program you're given with your ticket—it gives you the schedule of shows for the day.

• The general rule is that the scarier the ride, the more popular it is, so always aim to see the most intense attractions in the morning, when the park isn't as crowded. If your kids are young and you'll be skipping the coasters, begin with Bigfoot Rapids and Log Ride, then work your way down to the kiddie rides. But be sure to bring along extra T-shirts for the water rides no matter what time of the day you ride them. If your kids are older and you plan to ride the coasters, visit at least two of them before midmorning, then work your way down to the medium-intensity rides in the afternoon.

• If your kids are unsure about a ride, let them watch it first. Jaguar!, Boomerang, Log Ride, Windjammer, and Parachute Sky Jump are visible enough so that you can watch the ride make a few runs before deciding whether to try it. Montezooma's Revenge is partially obscured by the trees and is thus harder to gauge; although riders rate it less intense than Boomerang, it does make one breathtaking full-circle loop.

• Knott's really opens up in the middle of the park, which can be an uncrowded oasis in the heat of the afternoon. Stop by the church on the shores of Reflection Lake—it was built in 1876 and still holds services. Reflection Lake is also home to the Incredible Waterworks Show and nightly fireworks during the on-season. If everyone needs a break from touring, pick up some lunch at La Conchita or the Ghost Town Grill and have a picnic on one of the benches by the water.

• The Lost Children's Center is in the Information Center near the front gate, but it's unlikely that lost kids would find it on their own. Park employees are dressed like cowboys and cowgirls and thus stand out in a crowd. Instruct the kids to tell an employee if they get separated from you; the employee will take them straight to the Lost Children's Center. As mentioned before, it helps to attach a note to very young children, listing your name and hotel or home phone number in case the child is too young to know this herself.

• Concentrate on attractions that emphasize the California Gold Rush theme. If you'll be in other theme parks during your vacation, you'll undoubtedly have plenty of chances to ride a roller coaster, but how often do you get to pan for gold?

Touring Plan

1. Be at the front gate 20 minutes before the stated opening time.
2. If your kids are old enough to tackle the major coasters, head for Jaguar! first, then Montezooma's Revenge and Boomerang. If your kids are younger, veer left upon entering the park and begin with Bigfoot Rapids (the family white-water ride), then move on to the medium-intensity rides in the Roaring '20s and Fiesta Village sections of the park. Backtrack to Ghost Town in the afternoon when the kids need a rest.
3. Camp Snoopy sometimes doesn't open until mid-morning, so visit other parts of the park first. Once this kiddie section is open, it's rarely crowded, so youngsters can move among the rides, swinging bridges, and ball pits at leisure.

4. Have an early lunch—perhaps at the Grizzly Creek Lodge, where the Peanuts gang often hangs out for pictures and autographs—then head back toward the main gate.

5. If it's time for the first stunt show, proceed to the Wagon Camp. If not, cut through the middle of Ghost Town and ride the Stagecoach, Log Ride, and Calico Mine Train. Be prepared for a long wait for the Stagecoach, which, because of its size, takes a limited number of people at a time.

6. Spend the afternoon in the theater-style attractions, like Kingdom of the Dinosaurs, Mystery Lodge, the Toyota Good Time Theater, or the Dolphin and Sea Lion Show. Consult your entertainment schedule for show times.

7. At about 4 P.M., have your hand stamped, then exit the park for an early supper at the Chicken Dinner Restaurant, located among the shops of the nearby California Marketplace.

8. Reenter the park after you eat and make a final lap, riding anything you missed earlier.

Best Attractions

Here's a breakdown of the best rides for each age group.

Best Attractions for Kids 2 to 7
(Height minimums are indicated if required.)
> All the Camp Snoopy Rides
> Bigfoot Rapids (36 in.)
> Stagecoach ride
> Log Ride (check out that final drop first!)
> Wild West Stunt Show
> Kingdom of the Dinosaurs

Mexican Hat Dance (see "Scare Factor" above)
Merry-go-round and many Fiesta Village rides
Dolphin and Sea Lion Show
Mystery Lodge

Best Attractions for Kids 7 to 11
(Height minimums are indicated if required.)
    Jaguar! (42 in.)
    Most Fiesta Village rides and the Roaring '20s
    Bigfoot Rapids (36 in.)
    Stagecoach ride
    Log Ride
    Wild West Stunt Show
    Mystery Lodge
    Dolphin and Sea Lion Show
    Parachute Sky Jump
    Kingdom of the Dinosaurs
    Bumper cars
    Headache
    Boomerang (but watch it first!) (52 in.)
    Montezooma's Revenge (but watch it first!) (48 in.)
    Windjammer (but watch it first!) (48 in.)

Best Attractions for Teens and Preteens
(Height minimums are indicated if required.)
    Windjammer (48 in.)
    Jaguar! (42 in.)
    Montezooma's Revenge (48 in.)
    Boomerang (52 in.)
    Parachute Sky Jump
    XK-1
    Tampico Tumbler (52 in.)
    Log Ride   *(continued)*

Bigfoot Rapids (36 in.)
Wild West Stunt Show
Mystery Lodge
Dolphin and Sea Lion Show

Parades, Fireworks, and Shows

In the on-season Knott's offers specially themed parades and a nightly fireworks-and-fountain display over Reflection Lake.

The shows run year-round, including the Dolphin and Sea Lion Show. You can also visit the Calico Saloon for a shamelessly overwrought melodrama in which the crowd is encouraged to hiss the villain, cheer the hero, and swoon along with the maiden in distress. There are Native American folklore demonstrations in the Indian Trails section and musical presentations at the Toyota Good Time Theater. Kids can meet the Peanuts characters in Camp Snoopy and see a toddler-oriented animal show there. All the afternoon entertainment offers a chance to rest up from the morning touring.

Holidays are very special. If you're visiting in the weeks before Halloween, Knott's Berry Farm becomes Knott's Scary Farm and Halloween Haunt, filling the streets of Ghost Town with ghouls, goblins, and rolling blankets of fog. The shows and rides are revamped to a Halloween theme, and the park stays open past midnight. This ultimate spook party is popular with locals and is always a sellout—call 714-220-5220 to learn how to purchase your tickets well in advance. The Halloween Haunt is way too spooky for preschoolers, but kids 7 and older will love it.

The Easter EggMazeMent party (during which elaborately themed, walk-through adventure mazes are constructed) and the Knott's Merry Farm Christmas festivities (including Snoopy's Nutcracker on Ice) are also popular. Again, contact Information for details on special holiday activities, advance ticket purchases, and prices.

Afternoon Resting Places

As you'll probably be spending only a day at Knott's, it may not be feasible to leave midday and return. Concentrate instead on finding afternoon resting places within the park, such as at the Dolphin and Sea Lion Show; the Wild West Stunt Show (get there early for a shady seat); the Toyota Good Time Theater; the Mystery Lodge; the Kingdom of the Dinosaurs; the Nu Wave Theater; lunch at the Chicken Dinner Restaurant; a train or stagecoach ride; a wander through the Ghost Town and Indian Trails, savoring the shops, shows, and demonstrations; or a stop at Reflection Lake, a quiet, secluded place to nurse a beverage on a hot July afternoon.

Dining Tips

Walt Disney was fond of saying, "It all started with a mouse." At Knott's Berry Farm, it all started with a chicken, and sometime during your stay you should stop by Mrs. Knott's Chicken Dinner Restaurant. Leave the park by way of the Ghost Town exit, have your hand stamped, then cut through the shops of the California Marketplace. The Chicken Dinner Restaurant is accessible to both park-goers and the general public, and it's extremely popular, with lines forming from 11 A.M. on. The best time to go is around 3:30 to 4:30 P.M., perhaps after the midafternoon Wild West Stunt Show, when you'll be located conveniently near the gate.

A $9.95 dinner for adults includes soup, salad, four pieces of fried chicken, a vegetable, and mashed potatoes and gravy. The dinner concludes with a choice of boysen-berry or apple pie with ice cream or sherbet. The kids get soup, chicken, veggies, and dessert for $4.95. Make no mistake about it—this is quite a food bargain.

The Chicken Dinner Restaurant is casual and family oriented, and youngsters get crayons and Snoopy menus. Service is fast, and the waitresses bring hot homemade biscuits the minute you sit down. There's plenty of famous Knott's jam on the table.

The California Marketplace adjacent to the restaurant is a good place to shop for a variety of souvenirs. The jams, preserves, and syrups at the Knott's Farm Market make the perfect gift for teachers, grandparents, or the neighbors who are feeding the dog—but 12 boxed jars of jelly are heavier than you'd guess, so be sure to make this shop the very last stop as you exit. The Farm Market will also ship to your home.

CHAPTER *7*

*More
Orange County
Attractions*

RAGING WATERS

111 Raging Waters Drive, San Dimas
909-592-6453 for information

Depending on when you visit Southern California, the weather can be hot, hot, hot. That's the best time to visit Raging Waters, which is only about 30 minutes from downtown Los Angeles and Anaheim.

Water parks can be a lot of fun on those hot days, as long as you remember a couple of things: They can get extremely crowded, and children under 7 must be watched carefully. There are thrill water rides galore at Raging Waters, making it a great place for preteens and teenagers. But you won't need me to tell you what it's like for young children. You'll see for yourself on a hot weekend day that Splash Island Adventure and Volcano FantaSea become congested with youngsters slip-sliding their way from a fun spray fountain to mini water slides. Sometimes the older children get in the way. Plan to spend lots of time watching your toddlers (and even kids a bit older) so they don't get pushed under the water.

Raging Waters has more than 25 water rides, including a wave cove for body surfing, a lazy river for tubing, and of course slides. The thrills range in intensity from the Little Dipper kiddie pool with its gentle slopes to monster slides with names like Drop Out, Dark Hole, Vortex, and High Extreme. Flumes and slides come in varying heights and complexity, so kids of almost any age can find the right type of fun. But parents need to stay alert. I watched young children who were not strong swimmers get swept under the water at the bottom of a water slide. Lifeguards stationed at the finish of each ride were quick to scoop out struggling kids. There is also the ever present possibility that someone coming off a slide or out of a wave will crash into a child. But the guards were vigilant about preventing this. Access to attractions is strictly related to height; kids under 48 inches aren't allowed on the monster slides.

Now that all the dangers have been addressed, what about the fun parts? Kids of all sizes and shapes come down the slides laughing with glee and demanding a repeat performance. The lines for the popular slides can be long—20 minutes on average—and for some slides the wait is in the hot sun.

There's not much of a scare factor to worry about here; the consensus was that the water rides were fun, not scary. Vortex was a particular favorite. High Extreme was a long climb up for a ride down that was rated average, although the ride is made more exciting because riders travel headfirst down the 109-foot slides.

Remember that Raging Waters is open seasonally, so be sure to call for current hours. Admission is $22 for anyone 48 inches and taller; under that, it's $13. There are often coupons and discounts available at Los Angeles supermarkets and in newspapers. Parking is $5. Lockers cost $4 and $5 (plus deposit). There are changing rooms and showers. Lawn chairs, umbrellas, and lounging mats can be rented, as can tented cabanas ($40 for four chaise lounges). Tubes are free and provided on appropriate rides; life vests are also free.

Touring Tips

• It helps to get to Raging Waters early—at least 20 minutes before the stated opening time so you can park closer to the entrance, get tickets, grab lawn chairs in the shade, rent a locker, swab the kids with SPF 24, and be ready to hit the major slides when the gates open.

• Although there are shady resting areas, chaise lounges in those spots get grabbed up immediately, as does any shady spot on the grass.

• Be sure to wear rubber-bottomed shoes; this can be one slippery, hot place (although many folks go barefoot, others choose to hold on to their water shoes as they come down the slides).

• Raging Waters is kept quite clean for a place so full of wet people, and there are plenty of park employees walking around should you need assistance.

• Pizza seems to be the most popular park food, but there is a stand for burgers and salads and one for sandwiches. You'll find that drinks are expensive but that food prices are average.

WILD RIVERS WATERPARK

8770 Irvine Center Drive, Irvine
714-768-WILD for information

Wild Rivers Waterpark, located in Irvine between Laguna Beach and Newport Beach, has more than 40 water rides with an African jungle theme, many of them suitable for kids younger than 10. Preschoolers can try Pygmy Pond or the gentle inner tube float ride dubbed the Safari River Expedition. In new Tugboat Bay, they can scramble up the Crab Slide or pretend they're sailors on the Wild Rivers Tug. Older kids can tackle the water tubing, speed slides, tunnels, and two side-by-side wave pools, one offering body-boarding. As with any water park, no matter how safe it's touted to be, keep an eye on kids of all ages.

There are lockers, equipment rentals, and changing rooms here. Note that food and drinks can't be brought in, but there are food stands in the park and a public picnic area outside the park.

Wild Rivers is open from May to June on weekends and holidays. From the end of June to September 1, it's open daily from 10 A.M. to 8 P.M. Admission is $20 for adults and kids 10 and over, $16 for kids 3 to 9. Evening discounts go into effect in the summer, when the park stays open later. Parking is $4.

MOVIELAND WAX MUSEUM

7711 Beach Boulevard, Buena Park
714-522-1155

Movieland Wax Museum is a fun way to kill a couple of hours, and it's just a block from Knott's Berry Farm and an easy 15-minute drive from Disneyland. The wax figures here are a bit more contemporary than those in the Hollywood Wax Museum; the kids will recognize and enjoy the *Star Trek* and *Wizard of Oz* characters (even if they aren't sure who Brando, Hepburn, and Bogart are) as well as the newest members of the wax family: Little Richard, John Travolta, and Bruce Lee. The Chamber of Horrors is popular with teenagers and preteens, although it's probably too scary for preschoolers. As at the Hollywood Wax Museum, the gory stuff is off by itself and touring it is optional. Because of its location, the Movieland Wax Museum is a good stop to make after a visit to Knott's Berry Farm or on your way to see Medieval Times or Wild Bill's Wild West Show.

Admission is $13 for adults, $7 for kids 4 to 11. Many Anaheim-area hotels offer discounted tickets. It's also possible to get a combo ticket (adults $17, kids $10), which includes the adjacent Ripley's Believe It or Not! There's a silly sort of charm in seeing an eight-legged pig or the shoes of the tallest man in the world. Movieland and Ripley's can be a godsend on a rainy afternoon. Both are open every day of the year.

MEDIEVAL TIMES

7662 Beach Boulevard, Buena Park
800-899-6600 or 714-523-1100

This family-style dinner show in Buena Park transports you back to the year 1093. Dueling swordsmen and jousting knights on horseback compete in a medieval tournament in a huge arena as they hope to pay homage to the Queen while guests dine on roast chicken and ribs. This is entertainment suitable for the whole family, with substantial, no-frills dining and rowdy reveling. Kids love the chance to wear crowns, eat with their bare hands, and cheer for their favorite knights.

The cost is $34 for adults, $23 for kids 12 and younger. The prices are slightly higher on Saturday. Discount coupons are available, and many area hotels offer discounted tickets. The price includes the show, a hearty four-course meal, and beer and wine for the adults. Generally there are two seatings nightly in the high season and three seatings nightly on weekends. Although the arena seats just over 1,000, it's best to make reservations in advance. Medieval Times is only a 15-minute drive from Disneyland and a 5-minute drive from Knott's Berry Farm.

WILD BILL'S WILD WEST DINNER EXTRAVAGANZA

7600 Beach Boulevard, Buena Park
800-883-1546 or 714-522-6414 for directions,
hours, and reservations

Sometimes the hokiest shows are the most fun, and that could well be the case with this dinner theater. Wild Bill's offers rootin' tootin' gun-slingin' entertainment and country music while barbecued ribs, fried chicken, and corn on the cob are served up chuck-wagon style. Audience participation is encouraged (and there's plenty of audience in this 800-seat show room), especially during the "skills of daring" specialty acts. This is a two-hour extravaganza, so if you think the little ones won't make it, try a weekend matinee instead.

The cost is $34 for adults, $22 for kids 12 and younger. Prices are slightly higher on weekends and lower for matinees. Discount coupons are widely available, and many area hotels offer discounted tickets.

CHAPTER *8*

And Don't Miss...

UNIVERSAL STUDIOS HOLLYWOOD

Universal Studios is by far the most user-friendly of the Southern California theme parks, moving crowds quickly and allowing you plenty of chances to rest. You can tour the park in about six hours, not because there isn't plenty to do but because Universal has planned the show schedules so efficiently that you can move from attraction to attraction in smooth sequence, rarely encountering more than a 15-minute wait, except for the rides and a couple of the shows.

Details

Universal City, Hollywood
818-508-9600 for directions and information

Admission to Universal is $36 for adults, $26 for kids 3 to 11; two-day passes cost $48 for adults, $37 for children. There are numerous discount coupons available, and area hotels sometimes offer discounted tickets. Also, there are often promotional specials in the local supermarkets.

Universal, which is located high in the Hollywood Hills just north of Los Angeles, is open from 8 A.M. to 10 P.M. during summer and holiday seasons, 9 A.M. to 7 P.M. during the rest of the year. As the hours can change, call on the day you'll be visiting.

The parking lots are vast and serve Universal's CityWalk and the popular concert venue, the Universal Amphitheatre. If you're driving any type of recreational vehicle, you may be directed to a different parking lot. Be sure to write your location on your ticket and take it with you. Parking is $6.

Highlights

Universal's appeal lies not just in its rides (of which there are only three) but also in the shows and the famous Studio

Backlot Tram Tour, which re-creates exciting special effects from popular films. The theme park is situated in the middle of the actual studio backlot, and the tram tour goes through literally acres of filming locations. All around you are reminders that many of these are working sets with TV shows and movies in production daily.

The park's thrills are high-tech and, to be totally engaging, require at least some knowledge of the featured movie or TV show. Anyone can enjoy the Back to the Future ride, but fans of the film are apt to appreciate the in-jokes and special effects more. Perhaps for this reason, Universal is most popular with older school-age children, teens, and adults. Kids younger than 7 should be briefed in advance that this is not a typical theme park, as there are no merry-go-rounds or bumper cars to be found. Once they understand this, younger kids will have fun—especially on the E.T. ride or while watching the Animal Actors Stage Show, the Land Before Time Show, and the Wild, Wild, Wild West Stunt Show.

Between Back to the Future, Backdraft, Waterworld, and the Tram Tour, Universal packs some major punches and gives you the feeling of being on a real movie set—because you are. Perhaps this is why one of the families surveyed described it as "the most California of all the California parks."

The Rides

Universal Studios is divided into two levels: Studio Center (the lower level) and Entertainment Center (the entrance level). The Studio Tram Tour is accessed via an escalator from the entrance level.

The Studio Tram Tour

The 50-minute Studio Tram Tour, which leaves from a well-marked station near Back to the Future, is a must-do attraction. Go either early or late; lines peak between 11 A.M. and 3 P.M.

If it's not crowded, lines move quickly, and trams arrive one after the other. The Universal people are eager to please, so you can even eat and drink on the tram. The first part of the tour is tame, so you'll have time to eat before the real action begins.

Try to sit on the right side of the tram if you want to see Jaws and King Kong up close and personal. Once aboard, it's just a matter of sitting back and relaxing as the movies come to you. You'll start with a drive on the lot past important soundstages and some large outdoor sets, where TV series like "Murder, She Wrote" and films like *Back to the Future* were shot. (The neighborhood street where Andy Griffith, Beaver Cleaver, and the Munsters all "live" is a special treat for baby-boomer parents and kids hooked on "Nick at Nite.")

Your first stop is inside a soundstage in the New York section of the lot, where you'll confront King Kong, coming close enough to inspect his four-foot fangs and feel the hot blast of his banana-breath on your face. Then it's on to San Francisco and Earthquake, where inside a re-created subway station, the rumbles, fires, floods, and train wrecks brought on by a simulated earthquake will make you feel that you really are in the middle of *The Big One.* It's even more fascinating to watch the water recede, the concrete mend itself, and the fires implode when the quake is over!

As the tour continues, you'll meet up with the great-white star of *Jaws,* be swept away in a flash flood, and cruise the exterior of the Bates Hotel (who's that at the window?). Especially convincing optical illusions are found at Dante's Peak—although the tram never actually moves, you truly feel that you're spiraling backward.

Scare factor: Parents report that they were the most skeptical about the Jaws segment of the tour, but the truth is that the attack happens so fast that many kids never even see the shark. You're more apt to hear shrieks of disappointment than terror. King Kong, in contrast, is one big ape and hard to miss. The Earthquake "jolt" happens within a soundstage where it's fairly warm and close. For those of us who live in Southern California, it's pretty realistic. The 6-year-old boy I sat with claimed he wasn't scared, but his eyes told me otherwise. Prepare youngsters ahead of time, and they'll usually be okay. The effect of Dante's Peak is totally visual, but if it gets to you, just close your eyes.

All the special effects are quick (except Dante's Peak), and because you're in an open-air tram surrounded by lots of other people, the experience remains more fun than scary. Most young kids enjoy the tram tour, although the first 15 minutes they declared boring. (If a child does freak out during the Studio Tram Tour, the driver is prepared to let the family off. An employee will take you back to the tram station in a separate car.)

Studio Center (Lower Level)

To reach Studio Center (the level below the entrance), take the Starway Escalator (actually a long series of covered escalators) at the rear of the park. If you have a stroller or wheelchair in your party, take the elevator located just to the right of the Starway.

Jurassic Park—The Ride

If you've seen the movie, you know the premise. Visitors enter a world dedicated to cloning prehistoric animals. But instead of exploring this scary 3-D world by Jeep, as in the movie, you'll board huge river rafts. Realistic looking dinosaurs rise from the water and appear in the canyons, some looming up very close to the raft. Soon you find that the dinosaurs have escaped, and Jurassic Park seems to be falling apart. Just as a gargantuan T-Rex leans over to eat you, you plunge 84 feet down the rapids. Teenagers and even preteens love this ride. Your children younger that 7 might find it frightening. Bring a change of shirts—this is a wet one.

E. T. Adventure

E.T. is as technologically impressive and emotionally seductive as anything at Disneyland, and because there's nothing remotely scary about it, the entire family can enjoy the ride.

The attraction begins with a brief video featuring Steven Spielberg and E.T., after which you file through a holding area and—somewhat mysteriously at the time—are required to give your name in exchange for a small plastic "interplanetary passport." The queue winds through a deep dark wood so evocative that it even sounds and smells like a forest, with overpowering trees designed to make visitors feel small and childlike.

When you arrive at the ride, you hand over your passport to the attendant and climb aboard a bicycle. (Children under 42 inches tall, the elderly, the heavily pregnant, and the otherwise unsteady are loaded into flying gondolas instead.) The bicycles are grouped onto platforms, and E.T. sits in the front basket of the lead bike. You rise up and fly through the forest in an effective simulation of the escape scene in the movie and, after narrowly missing capture by the police, return E.T. to the Green Planet, a magical place full of cuddly, singing aliens.

The ride closes on a stunning note, for as you sail past E.T. for the final time, he bids you farewell by name. How? When you gave your name to the attendant way back in the holding area, it was computer coded onto your passport. When you gave up your passport and were loaded onto the bikes, the cards were fed into the computer, so the ride "knows" who is riding in that particular batch of bicycles. This enables E.T. to say "Good-bye Jordan, Good-bye Leigh" as your family sails past.

Unfortunately, the personal good-bye system sometimes malfunctions, so I wouldn't mention it to the kids at all. That way if it works, everyone is extra-delighted; if it doesn't, the ride is still an upbeat experience.

World of Cinemagic

This 30-minute show uses audience volunteers (or draftees if the crowd is timid) to illustrate special visual effects from *Back to the Future,* re-create the shower scene from *Psycho,* and dub sound effects into a clip from *Harry and the Hendersons.* The show is fast paced and funny, and you move from set to set, with a new tour group beginning the cycle every 10 minutes. If you'd like to be electrocuted on top of the Mill Valley Courthouse, roar like an ape, or be stabbed by Mother Bates, the key is to sit front and center in the first few rows and, when the tour leader asks for volunteers, shamelessly wave your arms. They aren't looking for shy people here. In fact, they seem to choose quite a few teens. Needless to say, the teenagers declare this a very "cool" attraction.

Scare factor: Even the Psycho part of the show is played for laughs, but if you have a child who might be unnerved by the scene, tell the attendant—it's possible to move through the central section of the show to Harry and the Hendersons, skipping the Psycho segment altogether.

Backdraft
Exciting and undeniably hot, Backdraft brings Ron Howard's movie to life with exploding barrels, falling beams, and 10,000 degrees of heat. In the final scene the entire room becomes engulfed in flames, and the bridge where you're standing suddenly jerks, as if threatening to give way and drop you into the furnace below. Preteens and teens like it best, although the final scene is brief enough that children younger than 10 shouldn't be too overwhelmed.

Like World of Cinemagic, you move from theater to theater, so a new tour group starts through every 10 minutes, and the line moves steadily. Still, come in the morning, as the afternoon can draw major crowds.

Scare factor: The final scene, when the room where you're standing is engulfed in flames, actually seems to alarm parents more than kids. Few families surveyed reported problems.

Lucy: A Tribute
Fans of "I Love Lucy" should take a few minutes to walk through this exhibit, which houses memorabilia from the famous TV series, including clothes worn on the show, personal pictures and letters from Lucy and Desi's home life, and the numerous Emmys that Lucille Ball won throughout the years. There's an engaging game to play called "California Here We Come." By answering questions about episodes of "I Love Lucy," game participants get to travel cross-country with the Mertzes and Ricardos on their first

trip to Hollywood. Children of many ages sit on the floor mesmerized by the "Lucy" scenes projected on a big screen.

Entertainment Center (Entrance Level)

Back to the Future
Flight-simulation technology makes a quantum leap forward—or is it backward?—in Back to the Future. After a preshow video, in which Doc Brown (played by Christopher Lloyd of the movie series) explains that bad-boy Biff has sabotaged his time travel experiments, you'll be loaded into six-passenger Deloreans; what follows is a high-speed chase through the prehistoric era. The cars bounce around quite a lot, but it's the flight-simulation techniques that are the real scream-rippers, far more intense than those provided by Disneyland's Star Tours. (Passengers who can bear to glance away from the screen will notice as many as 12 Deloreans, arranged in tiers, taking the trip simultaneously, making Back to the Future a sort of ultimate drive-in movie.)

At one point in your trip you're even swallowed by a dinosaur. The ride is a bit intense for kids younger than 7, although technically anyone over 40 inches is allowed to board. If your child does want to try the ride, remind him that many of the special effects can be avoided simply by closing his eyes—and that's not a bad tip to remember yourself if you're prone to queasiness. For those with strong stomachs, however, the ride is a pure pleasure, and it's one of the attractions at Universal that draws really horrific lines. Ninety-minute waits are typical in the afternoon, so ride Back to the Future first thing in the morning.

Scare factor: The visual effects in this ride are extremely convincing, and the car does bump around a lot; most kids

7 and older were cool with the ride, but think twice before taking on a preschooler, even one who passes the 40-inch height requirement. Once the ride begins, there's no way off and, because riders are packed into small Deloreans, no way to dilute the intensity of the experience except by shutting your eyes. There were a couple of reports of motion sickness among the families surveyed.

The Shows

Remember I mentioned you should hang on to the entertainment schedule you received as you entered the front gates? The shows start at the times stated on the schedule *or* as soon as the theaters are filled. Most of the theaters are so large that lining up 15 minutes in advance will assure you a seat, and the schedule is set up so that you can move from one show to another with minimal waits. Even with large-capacity seating, Waterworld and Totally Nickelodeon are so popular that people line up 20 to 30 minutes in advance.

Waterworld

Although it's only 15 minutes long, this is by far the most popular show at Universal, and you'll find hundreds of people lining up for it 30 minutes in advance. Based on the Kevin Costner movie of the same name, Waterworld is a series of 60 stunts using hovercraft, jet skis, cannons, catapults, pyrotechnics, and fireworks. It pits the bad guy, Deacon (who is surely one of the best show characters in the park), against the hero, Mariner, and the heroine, Helen. I hate to give the climax away, but if you're sitting in the middle of the first few rows, warn your little ones that something big will happen.

The theater is huge, and once you're in the queue, you are assured a seat. The green seats are for those willing to get splashed.

Scare factor: Parents have their own takes on what is or isn't too violent for their children to watch, and I don't want to make that decision for you. On the one hand, this show uses heavy-duty weapons and lots of fiery, realistic explosions. On the other hand, Deacon is actually quite humorous, and there's a strong female character. You'll have to be the judge of whether you want to take children under 11 to see the show.

Totally Nickelodeon

This 30-minute show is well worth standing in line for. Once you've seen it, you can forgive the fact that this is one giant commercial for the Nickelodeon TV station. The volunteers (that's you) get to choose which games they want to play from Nickelodeon shows such as "Family Double Dare" and "The Secret World of Alex Mack." If you want to volunteer to get gallons of slinky slime dumped on you from the Sliminator, try to be near the first one-fourth of the line. The audience is divided into teams; far from being passive viewers, they have plenty to do. It's all in good fun, and the adults really get into it.

Scare factor: This one is fine for any age. But the studio is huge, so be sure to hang on to your little ones when you exit.

Wild, Wild, Wild West Stunt Show

Funny, fast moving, and full of surprises, this show ranks high with kids 7 to 11 and even those younger than 7. The shoot-'em-ups, fistfights, and explosions are played in a broad comic style that sometimes overshadows how dangerous these stunts really are. The theater is big, so the show is easy to get in to, even during the most crowded part of the afternoon.

Scare factor: The noise of gunshots and the heat of the pyrotechnics is fairly intense. If you have a youngster who's sensitive to noise and sudden special effects, let him or her know about these elements of the show. You may want to sit higher in the bleachers to muffle the effects.

Animal Actors Stage Show

If your kids are strung out from a combination of 90-degree heat, man-eating dinosaurs, and simulated earthquakes, the gentle Animal Actors Stage Show will offer a welcome change of pace. The show features stunts performed by apes, birds, and Benji-like dogs. Kids in both the 4-to-7 and the 7-to-11 age-groups rated the animals very highly. Because the theater is large, this is another good choice for the afternoon. This show is a fun one to videotape and watch again later at home.

Beetlejuice's Rockin' Graveyard Revue

Raucous rock 'n' roll is performed by Dracula, the Wolfman, the Phantom of the Opera, and Frankenstein and his Bride in this revue, which is very popular with kids 7 to 11 and teens. Babies and toddlers may be spooked by the sheer volume of the music, but the show is so goofy and upbeat that kids 2 to 7 certainly won't be frightened by the ghouls. The jokes are teen and adult oriented, so the kids under 11 won't really understand them.

This is a high-tech show featuring pulsating lights, fog machines, synchronized dancing, and wry renditions of rock classics such as *You Make Me Feel Like a Natural Woman* performed by the Bride of Frankenstein. The show plays frequently, so getting in isn't too tough. Save it for the most crowded times in the afternoon.

The Land Before Time

This is one show that doesn't need a warning label. This gentle, sweet show is based on the movie of the same name and is especially good for children under 11. The theme of the adventure includes friendship, best friends, and being scared. The audience sings right along with costumed Little Foot, Cera, Petrie, and their friends.

Touring Tips

• Once you've entered the park, be sure to hold on to the brochure you were given. It includes not only a helpful map but also the schedule of all the shows and musical attractions as well as the times for the last tram and last rides.

• All the scheduled shows and Back to the Future are located on the level you entered. Down a separate escalator near Back to the Future is the Studio Tram. Down the Starway (more later) are two rides.

• Lockers and stroller and wheelchair rentals are available after you've entered the park.

• Be sure to have your hand stamped if you plan to leave to visit CityWalk or return the same day.

• A bulletin board at the park entrance posts the names of shows and movies taping that day, but you won't be able to get on the sets. As Universal is a working studio and not merely a theme park designed to look like a working studio, several films or TV shows are likely to be in production at any given time. If you'd like to see a show in production, pick up passes at the TV Audience Ticket Booth. The ticket booth also gives away free tickets to shows that will be taping at other locations in the Los Angeles area. (For more information on TV tapings, see Chapter 9.)

• If you're ever unsure about what to do next, go to the information board located at the top of the Starway. The board lists upcoming show times and the approximate wait times at rides all over the park, and the helpful attendants will give you suggestions on where to go next.

• Seeing more than two shows in a row can lead to burnout for young kids. Take a break by watching the Doo-Wop singers at Mel's Diner or the Blues Brothers near Carleon and Sons. Older kids will prefer the boardwalk-style games and amusements at Carnival Internationale in the Moulin Rouge section of the park.

• Universal's location in the Hollywood Hills affords great views. Put a quarter in one of the big binoculars stationed to overlook the valley and let the kids look for stars—the ones in the sky, that is.

• With so many shows, finding an afternoon resting place is easy. Touring Universal isn't very tiring, and if you arrive early and move steadily, you may have done the park by midafternoon. If so, visit CityWalk or return to your hotel for a swim and a rest.

• The Moulin Rouge area is often the least-crowded section of the park. Shop, eat, and take your bathroom breaks there.

• Always see the newest and most popular stuff first: Ride Jurassic Park first thing, and see the first Waterworld show of the day.

- If you're visiting in the summer, when the park stays open late, you can still see it all in six hours; if possible, tour in the morning, take a midday break, and return. If that isn't feasible, enter the park about 3 P.M. and reverse the recommended touring schedule, doing the shows and tram tour first and the rides last.

Universal Studios Touring Plan

1. Arrive 20 minutes before the stated opening time to allow plenty of time to park and get tickets, maps, and entertainment schedules.
2. Visit the Studio Center (lower lot) first and ride Jurassic Park and E.T. and visit Backdraft. Take the Starway up and take the tram, then get in some shows. Save Back to the Future for dinnertime, when the crowds often thin out. Ride the tram tour midmorning or after 3 P.M., but remember that it closes earlier than the rest of the park.
3. Try to ride the rides first and save the shows for the afternoon. After you've ridden the major rides, take in an early lunch or snack, then visit the shows.
4. In late afternoon either eat in the park or have your hand stamped and leave the park entirely. Universal's CityWalk, with a great selection of shops and cafés, is a mere stroll away.
5. Return to the park and see any shows you missed.

Best Attractions

Here's a breakdown of the best rides for each age group.

Best Attractions for Kids 2 to 7
    E.T. Adventure
    Animal Actors Stage Show
    The Land Before Time   *(continued)*

Totally Nickelodeon
Beetlejuice's Rockin' Graveyard Revue
Wild, Wild, Wild West Stage Show

Best Attractions for Kids 7 to 11
Back to the Future
Waterworld
The Land Before Time
E.T. Adventure
Studio Tram Tour
Backdraft
World of Cinemagic
Wild, Wild, Wild West Stunt Show
Animal Actors Stage Show
Beetlejuice's Rockin' Graveyard Revue
Totally Nickelodeon

Best Attractions for Preteens and Teens
Jurassic Park—The Ride
Back to the Future
Waterworld
Studio Tram Tour
Beetlejuice's Rockin' Graveyard Revue
World of Cinemagic
Blues Brothers
Doo-Wop singers
Backdraft
Wild, Wild, Wild West Stunt Show
Totally Nickelodeon

The Extras

There is nearly always a "star" or cartoon character hanging
around the entrance to the Emporium, signing autographs

and posing for snapshots. Be sure to stop by and meet Marilyn Monroe, W.C. Fields, or Frankenstein. The Blues Brothers put on really jammin' concerts throughout the day outside Carleon and Sons, and Doo-Wop belts out '50s classics from atop a red convertible at Mel's Diner. Show times are indicated in your entertainment schedule. (There are tables near the area where both the Blues Brothers and Doo-Wop perform, so you can eat while you listen. But the shows are popular, so stake out a table 15 minutes before the singers are scheduled to appear.)

Dining Tips

The food service at Universal is a cut above that of the other area theme parks, with a more sophisticated selection than you find at Disneyland. The best plan is to eat one "snack" meal and one "real" meal, using the tips below to help you make the best choice.

• For a late lunch or early dinner, visit Universal's CityWalk, just outside the main gate. It's full of cafés and casual eateries, including Wolfgang Puck Pizzeria, Hard Rock Café, and Gladstone's 4 Fish. There's truly something for everyone here, and, because there are so many restaurants jammed in a three-block area, the wait is rarely long.

• Want to stay in the park? Mel's Diner, where the '50s group Doo-Wop performs, is a good choice for lunch. Dedicated to the hangout made famous by the movie *American Graffiti,* Mel's offers burgers, onion rings, chili-cheese fries, and old-fashioned milkshakes. Kids too young to remember the movie, much less the decade being spoofed, will still love the roller-skating carhops, blaring jukeboxes, and chrome-plated decor.

• If your kids are addicted to fast food, get them one of the kids' lunches. Try a hot dog at the River Princess, a drumstick at Doc Brown's Fancy Fried Chicken, or grilled cheese at Mel's Diner.

• The Moulin Rouge section of the park is the least crowded and also has some of the best restaurants, including Crepe de Paris, where you can get an oriental, cajun, or Caribbean-style crepe created to your specifications within minutes.

Tip: Even if you buy your food elsewhere, consider carrying it to the uncrowded umbrella tables found in the Moulin Rouge courtyard.

• Doc Brown's Fancy Fried Chicken offers a solid (and fast) meal and a great view of the Hollywood Hills. If you'd like to take in the same vista while snacking, pick up one of the fruity frozen drinks (either alcoholic or virgin) at the Hill Valley Beverage Company.

• You can make a sundae to order at Caribbean Chill Yogurt; the strawberries-and-cream crepe at Crepe de Paris is also a good choice for dessert.

• Not only is it okay to eat in the outdoor shows like the Animal Actors Stage Show and the Wild, Wild, Wild West Stunt Show, but Universal actively encourages this by putting snack stands near the theater entrances and trash cans inside. (On a recent visit I even saw some hardy souls chowing down during the shark attack on the Studio Tram Tour.) If you're on a tight schedule, carry your lunch into one of the outdoor theaters and eat while watching the show.

Great Snapshot Locations

There are lots of great places for memorable photos. Try any of the following scenarios: with your head inside the mouth of Jaws, which hangs on display as you enter the Cape Cod section; vamping it up with Marilyn Monroe or Charlie Chaplin outside the Emporium; perched on the hood of the red convertible outside Mel's Diner; from the top of the Starway Escalator with the Hollywood Hills as a backdrop; or in front of the Apollo 13 space capsule used in the movie and located at the bottom of the first Starway escalator.

UNIVERSAL'S CITYWALK

Universal Center Drive, Universal City
818-622-4455

Located right outside of Universal (but not requiring an admission ticket) is CityWalk, a pedestrian promenade designed to represent a variety of popular L.A. streets. There's always plenty going on here—from street musicians and magicians to wax dipping and ice-skating (November to January only).

There are plenty of shops, including Captain Coconut's Toys, Upstart Crow bookstore and coffeehouse, and any number of candy and souvenir shops. (This isn't "serious" shopping, so don't look for shoes or clothes; this is "give the kids $5 and let 'em go wild" shopping.) B.B. King's Blues Club plays live music nightly, Wizardz Magic Club presents a reasonably priced dinner show, and there are over a dozen other places to eat, all of them casual, family oriented, and full of surprises. KWGB, for example, is a hamburger joint in a radio station setting. There's a live DJ and table phones so you can call in music and food requests. You can't miss the Hard Rock Café with it's 65-foot electric guitar. The Wolfgang Puck Café is a reasonably priced way to experience the Puck phenomenon. There are also seafood, Italian, Mexican, and Japanese restaurants.

MAGIC MOUNTAIN

About 30 minutes north of Los Angeles by way of I-5, you'll find the town of Valencia, home of Magic Mountain, where the rides—not the theme—are the attraction.

Magic Mountain *is* its big rides. Press releases boast that Magic Mountain has "the best 'track' record of any amusement park in California," and there are indeed eight killer coasters. The focus here is on building the biggest, the fastest, and the scariest. If your kids are above the 48-inch height requirement for the big coasters and they love scary rides, Magic Mountain may be their favorite stop of the whole trip. It scored the highest approval rating among teenagers and is a great favorite among locals, many of whom buy season passes.

Families with kids younger than 9 (or kids who don't care for coasters) should skip Magic Mountain. The shows are simple and the kiddie rides even simpler—the sort you could find at any fair or amusement park back home. Magic Mountain is for families whose focus that day is on rides.

Many families, of course, have children of various ages, and the older kids may insist on spending a day at Magic Mountain. There are actually four levels of rides here—the terrifying, the moderately wild, the kiddie rides, and the water rides—so you should be able to keep younger kids entertained while the older ones tackle the major attractions. Keep in mind that the rides here are considerably wilder than any you have encountered or will encounter at

Disneyland or Knott's Berry Farm. Use the descriptions to help decide what is right for whom.

Details

Magic Mountain Parkway, Valencia
805-255-4111, 805-255-4100, or 818-367-5965,
818-992-0884

Current prices are $35 for adults, $17 for kids under 48 inches. Because price is determined by height, you might end up paying full price for your 7-year-old "adult," so Magic Mountain can get expensive fast. You can purchase a "combo" ticket for entrance to both the rides and Magic Mountain's water park next door, Hurricane Harbor; the price is $50 for adults, $17 for kids. There are numerous discount coupons in area magazines, and many hotels sell discounted tickets. Parking is $6.

Magic Mountain is open daily from May to November but only on weekends and holidays the rest of the year. Call to confirm hours (which vary widely).

The Rides

Magic Mountain is mammoth, with 10 different "lands," each a minivillage containing rides, midway games, food stands, and some welcome shade.

Following are highlights of each of the lands, with descriptions of what are considered the most popular, albeit terrifying, rides in the park. All these rides have strictly enforced height requirements and are appropriate only for kids 9 and older. The coasters are placed far apart from each other within the park, and waits can be long—up to two hours per ride on a busy day in summer for the most popular rides. So explain to the kids that, if they have visions of riding all the coasters, (1) an early start is mandatory, (2) you'll have to hustle from ride to ride, and (3) you still may not make it. Prepare to choose four or five from the group and focus on them.

Intense Rides

The newest of the new lands is Samurai Summit, home to Superman the Escape, billed as "the tallest, fastest thrill ride on the planet." In fact, the *Guinness Book of World Records* has pronounced Superman the world's tallest and fastest. So that said, imagine a 415-foot structure (that's 41 stories) with a car that travels straight up at 100 miles an hour in 7 seconds. The brave then experience 6.5 seconds of weightlessness at the top, followed by a backward free-fall. The wait for this popular attraction can be two hours long on a busy day. The height restriction is 48 inches.

You'll also find Ninja up here, a good first-time coaster for kids unsure about these rides. Like Batman (following), you dangle beneath the track; unlike Batman, at least this time you have a car. Ninja has stomach-churning side-to-side movement. The height requirement is 42 inches.

The next most popular ride with teenagers is Batman, located in the Gotham City Backlot, the most visually interesting of all the lands. Riders are suspended from below the track with nothing beneath their dangling feet but air. But far scarier than that are the hairpin turns, corkscrews, vertical loops, and a couple of moves that flip you literally head over heels. The wait in line is long here, too, and a good part of that wait is in the hot sun. Batman has the highest height requirement—54 inches. The 13-year-olds and adults surveyed thought this was a pretty "awesome" ride.

Baja Ridge is where you'll find Viper and Revolution, two looping coasters. One 10-year-old I spoke to found Viper scarier than Revolution. It's the world's largest looping coaster, with three loops, a corkscrew, a boomerang, an 18-story drop, and a pace of 70 miles an hour, nearly twice the speed of Space Mountain at Disneyland. Viper also has a height requirement of 54 inches. Revolution was the first coaster in the country to offer a 360-degree loop. Its height requirement is 48 inches. The wait for each of these two rides averages 45 minutes.

Not far from the gentle Grand Carousel in Six Flags Plaza is Flashback, so named because, as you ride, your life flashes before your eyes. This coaster incorporates six hairpin turns at a 180-degree angle. Translated, that means you drop face-first toward the ground six times within 90 seconds. Sound like fun? Anyone 48 inches and over can ride.

Cyclone Bay is Magic Mountain's answer to a California beach town. Here's where you'll find Psyclone, a wooden coaster designed in the spirit of Long Island's Coney Island Cyclone. There are 11 big hills in all, including one 95-foot drop. The height requirement is 48 inches. For an additional fee you can try out Dare Devil, a combination of skydiving and bungee jumping. You're cranked 150 feet off the ground and then swung at speeds reaching 60 miles an hour. They only take reservations here, and the extra cost runs $15 to $25 per person (you can go single, double, or triple).

The most beautiful roller coaster at the park is Colossus, which you see from the parking lot. It sits all by itself in Colossus County Fair. Colossus is a dual-track white wooden coaster with emphasis on speed and size. It's especially fun after dark! The height requirement is 48 inches.

Goldrush and Freefall are found in Monterey Landing. Goldrush is a runaway mine train, much like Big Thunder Mountain Railroad at Disneyland. It's tame enough for younger kids. The height requirement is 48 inches. Freefall is not really a coaster, but it's really popular with teenagers. Many of the people surveyed described it as "wilder than I bargained for." There's a single, intense 10-story drop at 55 miles an hour, making it the longest two seconds of your life. The height requirement here is also 48 inches.

Scare factor: Make no mistake about it: The rides above, for the most part, are designed to scare you speechless, and they succeed. Superman is the most intense ride, followed by the coasters. They are only for the very bold. The mildest coasters are Gold Rusher and Ninja, both good tests for kids who aren't sure if they can handle the bigger rides. Revolution, Flashback, Psyclone, Colossus, and Free Fall are somewhere in between.

Medium-Intense Rides

The park also has many medium-intensity rides, which are really updated versions of the midway rides parents remember from their youth—now with fancy new names. No longer merely Scramblers, Tilt-a-Whirls, or Bumper Cars, these new Buccaneers and Sandblasters still provide a lot of old-fashioned fun.

Kids 7 to 11 will also enjoy the water rides, listed separately. If they want to try the big rides, let them begin with Ninja or Gold Rusher, the mildest of the coasters.

Kiddie Rides

Bugs Bunny World has 13 rides to keep this age-group entertained. Although the attractions are simple and low-tech, kids accustomed to 40-minute waits at Disneyland will be thrilled to find they can board ride after ride without fighting crowds. The Looney Tunes characters appear in Bugs Bunny World in the afternoon for pictures, autographs, and a simple stage show with lots of audience participation. Preschoolers will also enjoy visiting real-life critters in the Animals in Action Show. For inquisitive youngsters there's a petting zoo with the ubiquitous goats that never fail to fascinate.

If older kids in this age-group are offended by the babyish mood of Bugs Bunny World, check out the 7-to-11 list and the list of water rides that follows. Many of these will be fine for 5- and 6-year-olds, assuming a parent rides with them. The height restriction on all of the water rides is 42 inches.

Water Rides
The water rides *in* the park are designed to be enjoyed by the whole family. You'll see everyone from 4-year-olds to teenagers to grannies in the queue. Prepare to get *very* wet.

Roaring Rapids, in Rapids Camp Crossing, is one of those very wet rides—white-water rafting in boats seating 12. This is a great family ride, but be prepared for a wait of up to 90 minutes.

Tidal Wave can be found in Monterey Landing. This water-flume ride plunges over a 50-foot waterfall, resulting in an equally giant splash.

Log Jammer, in High Sierra Territory, and Jet Stream, in Cyclone Bay, are both log flumes. The waits usually aren't too long for these rides.

Yosemite Sam's Sierra Falls, also in High Sierra Territory, is a fun raft ride with 760 feet of water slides.

Scare factor: The water rides are all pretty mild and okay for kids 5 to 11 (who don't mind getting splashed) and the older kids. The height requirements for the medium-intensity rides provide a pretty good gauge of just who should board what.

The Shows

The shows at Magic Mountain are always subject to change, often seasonal, and never up to the standards at Disneyland and Universal. Take in a show if you're looking for a chance to rest or for a cooling stop.

The two exceptions to this rule are the popular Batman Forever Stunt Show and Batman Nights—the laser, fireworks, and special effects extravaganza that closes the park during the summer.

Touring Tips

• Magic Mountain is so large and major attractions are so far apart that it's unrealistic to suggest that anyone except teenagers make several laps of the park. You'll be forced to visit attractions more or less in sequence with as little backtracking as possible.

• Kids 3 to 6 who could manage without a stroller at Disneyland or Universal Studios will more than likely need one here. The terrain is hilly, and it may seem tough to push a 50-pound kindergartner up Samurai Summit—but if the alternative is carrying the child, you'll be glad you have a stroller.

• Magic Mountain is not easy to get around. The maps are confusing, and there are few signs to lead you where you want to go. Areas like Samurai Summit and the path leading to Revolution and Viper are hilly. Although there is a monorail and gondola-like transport, they're not easy to find. What's worse, once you're on the monorail, there are no signs to tell you where you've stopped. The young adults tending the monorail rattle off information fast and furious on a poor microphone—it's very difficult to understand what they're saying.

• Although lines are long, be heartened by the knowledge that the preteens and teens surveyed felt the waits were worth it; the rides aren't just a brief lap around a small track—they're relatively long, at least for coasters. You're also entertained while you wait; monitors overhead run Looney Tunes cartoons, music videos, comedy shows, and sports highlights. To keep guests from swooning in the heat, some of the lines have overhead water misters.

• Keep in mind that this is the desert, and temperatures can climb dangerously high on a summer afternoon. The lines for several of the major rides (see descriptions above) are completely exposed to the sun. In the morning buy the kids a $4.25 drink in a sports bottle; the bottles are a practical souvenir, and the cost of a refill ($1.85) is cheaper than continually buying individual drinks. It's impossible to take in too many fluids while visiting this park—kids should keep drinks with them while waiting in line.

• Also because this is the desert, it can get cool in the evening. Dress in layers. Families who will be touring late should stash jackets in a locker or in the trunk of their car. As looney as this idea seems at 3 P.M., you'll be glad you have them by 10 P.M.

• By arriving before 10 A.M., you should be able to ride two or three of the major rides without much of a wait, but *don't* try to ride all the coasters before lunch—it's much too much. Take in a couple of coasters, then switch to a water ride or medium-intensity ride.

- This large and confusing park would be an awful place to lose a toddler. But if you do, contact a park employee immediately. Park employees know to intercept lost little ones and escort them back to Guest Relations, so the odds are good your child is waiting for you there.

- If you allow older kids and preteens to tour on their own (and they should be at least 13 before they're let loose here, and never with less than two kids together), set a meeting place, such as the Valencia Falls Pavilion, a lovely waterfall near the main gate. Separated parties can also leave messages for each other at Guest Relations.

Touring Plan

1. Call Magic Mountain the day before you visit to confirm operating hours. The park generally doesn't open until 10 A.M., so predawn rising isn't necessary. Allow plenty of time for the drive, however, as Valencia is 30 minutes from Hollywood and 90 minutes from Anaheim.

2. The cars begin to line up about 9:30 A.M. The parking lot is huge and far from the entrance. The later you are, the farther away you are. In summer, this is a very hot parking lot with no shade.

3. There are two ways to "do" the park. One way is to head for Superman or Batman first. They are so obscenely popular that they often have two-hour waits even when the other park coasters are posting waits of 20 minutes. From one or the other, begin to move in a counterclockwise direction around the park, stopping at the other coasters as you come to them.

    If you're more interested in medium-intensity rides, begin with the water rides and whatever smaller coasters you think your kids can handle. Then work your way in sequence around the park, taking in the medium-intensity rides listed in the order you find them.

If your kids are young, begin with the water rides, then move on to any medium-intensity rides you think are appropriate. Ride the bigger stuff during your first two hours in the park; Bugs Bunny World often opens after the rest of the park, and even when it is open, it's never too crowded. Save it for the afternoon.

The second way to do the park is to simply take your chances and begin to the left of the entrance, at Baja Ridge, where you'll find Viper and Revolution, then simply make your way around the park clockwise, ending with Flashback in Six Flags Plaza.

4. After riding as many rides as your stomach can handle, take a break. Magic Mountain is so far from Los Angeles that it's impractical to suggest returning to your hotel for a rest. Some options are to leave the park for a picnic in the small picnic area near the parking lot or visit Mooseburger Lodge, head for Hurricane Harbor (see below), or take in an early show.

    Magic Mountain is unbearably hot and can get quite crowded in midafternoon, so even if you opt to remain in the park, limit walking and find some shade.

5. If you're staying until closing and wish to see Batman Nights, there's no way to avoid being caught in the departing masses. Take a final bathroom break and buy souvenirs or snacks before the show, then try to sit on the aisle and near an exit. If you're too poky leaving the park, be prepared for a traffic jam in the parking lot.

Best Attractions

Here's a breakdown of the best rides for each age group.

Best Attractions for Kids 7 to 11
(Height minimums are indicated if required.)
  Atom Smasher (42 in.)
  Circus Wheel
  Grinder Gearworks (42 in.)
  Jolly Roger
  Sandblasters (42 in.)
  Scrambler (36 in.)
  Sierra Twist (42 in.)
  Spin Out (36 in.)
  Swashbuckler (42 in.)

Best Attractions for Preteens and Teens
  All the roller coasters
  All the water rides

Dining Tips

• The food at Magic Mountain is typical amusement park fare: hamburgers, hot dogs, pizza, and sandwiches. Families with picky eaters will do best at Food Etc., an air-conditioned fast-food court with a little something for everyone. Otherwise, just grab whatever looks fast and avoid *all* the food places between 1 P.M. and 3 P.M., when you may find yourself waiting 30 minutes. There's a McDonald's in Cyclone Bay (open seasonally).

• The one exception to the fast-food plague is Moose-burger Lodge, a sit-down restaurant with a fun Mounties-and-forests-and-plaid-shirts sort of theme. The Lodge offers a continuous buffet at lunch and dinner as well as items off the menu, such as the house special, the "mooseburger" (so named because it's huge), and chocolate "moose" for dessert. Your waiters are dubbed "the singing server scouts" for reasons that will soon become obvious. Mooseburger Lodge is a good choice if you want an afternoon break.

• There's really no reason to leave the park for food. On a busy day, just the walk to and from your car can be 10 or 15 minutes, and then you have to wait in the car line to get back in.

HURRICANE HARBOR

Magic Mountain Parkway, Valencia
805-255-4111

Directly adjacent to Magic Mountain is its water park, Hurricane Harbor, with 22 water rides for all ages. The newest is Black Snake Summit. Picture a 75-foot-tall tower connecting five water slides (two of which are the tallest in Southern California), and you've got the picture. Black Snake and Reptile Ridge (two open body slides and three enclosed—one with a straight drop of 70 feet) are the only two rides with 48-inch height requirements.

Castaway Cove, reserved for youngsters under 54 inches, contains the kiddie rides, which consist of small water slides and waterfalls, squirting objects, and a fortress with swings and slides. Nearby Octopus Island has a big beastie that is perfect for climbing. Shipwreck Shores, a family interactive area, is also a stroll away. River Cruise, a lazy floating river that encircles a reef, is a good family activity. Just wade out, find an inner tube, climb aboard, and relax. If you're up for wild water, try Lost Temple Rapids, the six-person white-water-rafting ride.

Although many of these activities are said to be geared to the whole family, parents should always use caution at any water park. One 6-year-old boy attempted the family-oriented wave pool, where he was knocked over by the two-foot-tall waves. None of the park employees helped him, even though it was obvious he couldn't stay on his feet. Luckily, his parents were close enough to scoop him out. Many water parks, not just Hurricane Harbor, have these types of wave pools. No matter what the signs say about height, it's always the best idea for parents to join young children in these activities.

Although Hurricane Harbor is bound to be swamped in the afternoon, it will still be a good respite from touring in the park.

Combination tickets may be purchased with your Magic Mountain ticket. The park houses snack bars and raft rentals; men's and women's changing rooms and showers are available, as are lockers. The park is open only in the summer and on selected spring and fall weekends. Hours vary, so call 805-255-4111 to confirm times on the date you'll be visiting.

The combo ticket costs $50 for adults, $17 for kids; admission to Hurricane Harbor only is $18 for adults, $11 for kids under 48 inches.

CHAPTER 9

What to Do
in Los Angeles

The Los Angeles area is really made up of many inviting neighborhoods. Although it's spread out, you can drive from one area to the other with relative ease, as long as you don't begin—or return—during rush hour. Remember to stash some snacks and water bottles in your rental car for those times you can't help but be stuck in traffic.

You can combine many of the following sites with a visit to Anaheim. Although you can tour Los Angeles and stay in an Anaheim hotel, you'll be doing a lot of driving. We suggest you divide your time; at the end of this chapter, you'll find some L.A.-area hotel suggestions.

Hollywood and Beverly Hills are often the first areas that folks think about when they make their travel plans. But you'll miss out on some wonderful family activities if you limit yourselves to just those sites.

TIPS FOR TOURING HOLLYWOOD

No matter how seedy Hollywood gets, it holds a constant fascination for visitors from all over the world. Although Sunset Boulevard is famous, too, if you're looking for the famous Walk of Fame, Hollywood Boulevard is what you're looking for. The sidewalk stars can be found from La Brea Avenue to Vine Street (at Vine, look north to the Capitol Records building, built to emulate a stack of 45-rpm records).

There are numerous public parking lots around Hollywood. Expect to pay $4 to $6 for all-day parking. You can also pay by the hour, but the way the rate is rigged you may be better off with the all-day rate even if you're just planning to stay a couple hours.

Hollywood can get downright lurid after dark. It's best to go during the day and stick to the area near Mann's Chinese Theater.

Make your first stop the Los Angeles Visitor Information office in Janes House at 6541 Hollywood Boulevard (closed Sunday) or call 213-689-8822. There, you can purchase a map of the Walk of Fame and get other details about the area. The Walk of Fame is made up of 2,000 stars— Marilyn Monroe's is right outside the funky McDonald's. The Walk of Fame may be somewhat of a misnomer as 99% of the names won't be remotely familiar to kids younger than 10, and about half of them won't mean anything to you either. But spotting Snow White, Clark Gable, or Elton John can be a kick.

One of the most fun things to do in Hollywood is to see a movie. The velvet-draped Egyptian Theatre is currently under renovation to restore it to its former opulence, but in the meantime El Capitan and Mann's Chinese Theater will transport you back to the days when going to the movies was a glamorous outing. The beautifully restored El Capitan shows first-run Disney releases, making it a good choice for families. Look ahead and to your right just as you exit for a terrific view of the famous Hollywood sign. Not into nostalgia? The Hollywood Galaxy, a new cinema that's so high-tech you'll feel you're inside a pinball machine, is also a great place to spend a rainy afternoon.

Mann's Chinese Theater is the most famous landmark of Hollywood. Legend has it that Norma Talmadge, an actress in the 1930s, accidentally stepped in some wet cement while attending a premier, and thus began the tradition of stars leaving their handprints and footprints outside the theater. It's fun to compare your foot size to John Wayne's, and Mann's is a great place to take snapshots.

Located in the Hollywood Galaxy complex is the Hollywood Entertainment Museum, an essential addition to Hollywood. If you've ever wondered what they do with some of the props from former TV shows, wonder no more. Among the many props are the bar from the TV show "Cheers," memorabilia from "Star Trek," and items from the old Max Factor museum. The museum is open Tuesday through Sunday; admission is $7.50 for adults, $4 for kids 5 to 12.

If you want to take a guided bus tour of the movie stars' homes, stop by Janes House or the Mann's Chinese theater to buy tickets for Starline Tours (213-463-3333). You can take a two-hour tour of the movie stars' homes (adults $29, kids $20) or a five-hour grand tour of Los Angeles (adults $49, kids $32). Call ahead, and they may even pick you up at your hotel. Discount coupons are literally blowing all over Hollywood. The buses leave frequently, and reservations aren't necessary. Even with the discounts, the tours are still a pricey venture and quite skippable. Few 6-year-olds will swoon at the chance to see the home of Gene Kelly or Doris Day, and four hours on a bus stalled in L.A. traffic can quickly become a nerve-wracking experience. But don't rely instead on those "maps to the stars' homes" hawked along Sunset Boulevard. The heroes of your children's generation are more likely living out in Malibu—or on a ranch in Wyoming or a farm in Virginia.

The Hollywood Wax Museum (213-462-8860) is entertainingly campy (adults $9, kids $7). The museum is perhaps best known for its Chamber of Horrors, a section devoted to screen monsters and a few real-life badniks. These full-size vampires and mummies can spook the willies out of young kids, but the exhibits are designed so that a trip through the Chamber is optional. If you're not sure the kids can handle it, one parent can quickly walk through, then return with the verdict. The Guinness Book of World Records (213-463-6433) across the street offers up its own kitsch, and there's a combo ticket (adults $13, kids $9) if you want to see both Guinness and the wax museum. Ripley's Believe It or Not! (213-466-6335), a weird hodge-podge of odd "stuff," is on the corner (adults $9, kids $6).

Shopping in Hollywood is proof that tacky can be fun; the streets are lined with souvenir shops full of movie memorabilia. If you'd like to have a picture of yourself cuddling up with Marilyn Monroe, an Oscar with your name engraved on it, a James Dean pencil sharpener, or an Elvis sno-globe, you've come to the right place.

Obviously, many of the activities listed above are well suited for a rainy day, so if you encounter bad weather, head for Hollywood, the movie theaters in Westwood, and the area museums, where you can spend most of the day indoors. Also, Hollywood is most entertaining for children at least 10 years of age, who are old enough to "get" the nostalgia.

You can comfortably see the Hollywood area in two to three hours, assuming that you don't take one of the bus tours of the movie stars' homes. (If you do sign up for a bus tour, allow more time.) After you leave Hollywood, you'll be well placed to head west on Sunset Boulevard to Rodeo Drive and Beverly Hills. Or if the kids are all toured out, keep driving and spend the afternoon at the beach in Santa Monica.

TIPS FOR TOURING BEVERLY HILLS

If you take Sunset Boulevard from Hollywood to get to Beverly Hills, you'll pass through an entirely different world. Sunset Plaza and beyond is a world of outdoor cafés, European designer shops, intriguing billboards, and buildings covered in art. Sunset is also home to some of the famous music clubs, like Whisky-a-Go-Go, where some of the most celebrated rock stars in history have played.

Beverly Hills is only a half-hour drive west on Sunset Boulevard from Hollywood, but the two areas are light-years apart in mood. You can drive through the hills north of Sunset to see the beautiful houses, but there aren't too many children who will want to do that. Instead, jump on the Beverly Hills trolley in downtown Beverly Hills at Dayton Way and Rodeo Drive. There's a 40-minute tour, Sites and Scenes, makes a loop through the retail area and past some of the gorgeous homes in the residential area ($5 adults, $1 kids). It's more likely your children will enjoy this one because they'll be able to ride the open-sided green-and-gold tram. Its hours vary, so call 310-285-2438 for information.

The other "thing to do" here is stroll the famous shopping street of Rodeo Drive. There are numerous public parking places around Rodeo Drive where you can park for the first two hours free. Contact the Beverly Hills Visitors Bureau (800-345-2210 or 310-248-1010) for more information.

It is always fun to window-shop at Tiffany's, check out the jewels at Harry Winston, or take a peak into Gucci. Unless you're flush with money, it's strongly recommended that you not take kids younger than 10 into the shops, where a slight mishap could set you back thousands.

Along the way stop for a milk shake at Johnny Rocket's or, if you come at off-hours, dessert at the Cheesecake Factory, which has an unparalleled selection of sweets.

Holiday time is a beautiful time to explore the Golden Triangle (as it is called). You may even see a star doing her gift shopping or a limousine or two pull up in front of Polo or Chanel with—who knows?

TIPS FOR TOURING THE BEACHES

Let's face it: Touring a theme park is no day at the beach. At least once during your stay in Southern California you deserve a real day along our famous coast.

Select a beach with a pier; the presence of a pier usually means public parking ($4 to $6), restrooms, sidewalks, and playgrounds as well as places to buy snacks or rent bikes and roller blades. The Santa Monica Pier goes further (see "Santa Monica" below), offering rides, midways, shops, and seafood restaurants. In addition to the Santa Monica pier, beaches farther south have piers: Venice, Redondo Beach, Newport Beach, Hermosa Beach, and Manhattan Beach. Redondo and Santa Monica are by far the most bustling.

Santa Monica and Malibu are easily accessed from Los Angeles and are good choices on a day when you've toured Hollywood or Beverly Hills in the morning. If you're coming from Anaheim, a visit to Newport, Balboa, or Redondo Beach is in order.

An afternoon at the beach is a good finale to a day of touring, so consider going after you've spent time at a museum or zoo. There are changing areas at the public beaches, so if you put a tote bag with swimsuits and towels in the car before you leave in the morning, you won't have to return to your hotel. Remember that on a weekend in summer, the Pacific Coast Highway will be jammed at the end of the day. It's best to stay a bit longer than the crowds or to leave before 4 P.M.

If you'd prefer to visit a more private beach, the sort of place where the locals go, simply ask the desk clerk at your hotel for suggestions. Every Southern Californian has his or her favorite haunt and is only too happy to tell you why.

The smaller beaches tend to be quieter and more relaxing; the major drawback is often there's nowhere convenient to park.

Leo Carillo State Beach in Malibu is a great place to explore tide pools and sea caves. Zuma Beach, farther north, is a hot spot for teens in the summer. One of our favorites is Will Rogers State Beach at Pacific Coast Highway and Temescal Canyon because it's convenient, there's a lifeguard station, restrooms, a snack bar, and swings.

If you go to one of the large public beaches, be sure to take your stroller. Paved sidewalks run parallel to the water, and it's much easier to push toddlers than to lug them and their toys across acres of sand. Bikes, tandem bikes, and even bikes that pull small wagons designed for infants can be rented. Roller skates and roller blades are also widely available for rental, but unless you're already steady on your wheels, this is no place for you—the locals take this seriously!

The major beaches offer a variety of sports activities: volleyball nets, public playgrounds, and sidewalks for joggers. The sport you probably won't opt to pursue, ironically, is swimming. Depending on where you go, the water may not be clean. Watch for signs. The beaches farther north of Santa Monica, like Zuma, are better for swimming. Keep very close tabs on the kids if they're wading, as the waves can be rough.

Marina del Rey's manmade harbor is filled with pleasure boats, some of which can be rented.

Marina Boat Rentals	310-574-2822
Rent-a-Sail	310-822-1868

Whichever beach you select, save time for a drive up the Pacific Coast Highway (Highway 1), locally known as the

PCH. If you pick up the PCH in Santa Monica and drive north to Malibu and beyond, you'll experience the California coast everyone dreams of, with enormous rocks jutting dramatically up from the sea, winding roads clinging to the sides of mountains, and stunning sunsets over the dark-blue water. Stop for dinner at Gladstone's 4 Fish or Malibu Sea Lion, where the views are terrific.

Tip: If you have an extra day or two, continue up the PCH to Santa Barbara, a lovely seacoast town on the edge of Southern California's wine country. The beach is protected by a harbor, there's a wonderfully funky shopping district, or you could take a day-trip out to the vineyards.

SANTA MONICA

Minutes away from LAX and Beverly Hills, this ultimate California beach city earns its right to a closer study on the strength of its ambiance. It's easy to get there—west on the Santa Monica Freeway (10) will take you right to the water. But it's best to exit at Fourth or Fifth Street to get to the heart of Santa Monica and the pier. In the summer, parking is tricky—there are parking lots along Ocean Avenue and the PCH as well as municipal parking lots and beach parking. For beach parking, follow the bright orange and blue signs.

The venerable Santa Monica pier has re-created itself. The old-fashioned, tacky beach shops, sno-cones, and beer joints are gone. The pier (which has its own limited parking) has a carnival atmosphere, and on weekends the air is filled with many languages. Street artists vie for attention with entertainers and palm readers, all seeking "donations." The new Pacific Park lights up the nighttime sky with a giant Ferris wheel. The 11 midway rides can be experienced in about an hour. There are a few easy rides for young children, such as mini bumper cars and a swinging ship as well as a very gentle roller coaster. The arcade is typical—small and crowded with Skee Ball games, video machines, foosball, air hockey, and a few "virtual" games. There's round-the-clock security. Entrance to Pacific Park is free; the games average $1 to $3. There's a well-priced Mexican restaurant and a few food stands for drinks and fast food at the end of the pier, perfect for catching a Southern California sunset.

A huge expanse of beach extends on either side of the pier, with long sidewalks perfect for strolling and observing the tattoo-covered bodybuilders, blonde teenage girls, rollerblade whiz-kids, and other denizens of L.A. beach culture. Muscle Beach? I wouldn't plan to swim here—there are other beaches where the water is cleaner. A bike path starts north at Will Rogers Beach and runs south for about 22 miles. After playing on the beach, you can head back to the pier for a hot dog or venture a couple of blocks inland to the cool Third Street Promenade, an open-air pedestrian mall where much of the café dining is casual and alfresco. Third Street Promenade is a great place to people-watch. There are cafés with sit-down service, fast stops such as the famous Benita's Frites touting the best french fries in the world, yogurt shops, and a self-service food court offering Cajun, Mexican, Middle Eastern, and even Wolfgang Puck's Italian choices. Weekend nights bring out about every type of street entertainer you can imagine. Many of the stores stay open late. Your teenagers will probably like Urban Outfitters; there are shoe stores galore, bookstores, and two multiscreen movie complexes. Remember that this area gets especially congested in the evening. I wouldn't feel comfortable letting young teenagers off on their own on the Promenade, except in the movie theaters.

You may have heard that Arnold Schwarzenegger's restaurant is here. It's actually on Main Street, another area of Santa Monica good for walking. If your family chose a day on the beach or bike path, Main Street isn't far away. There aren't many things for young children to do on the street, but it makes a nice evening walk if you're in the area. Upscale, world-renown restaurants such as Chinois and Rockenwagner are located here. But if you're with the family, try Jake and Annie's or Lula's Cocina Mexicana.

CATALINA ISLAND

Twenty-two miles off the coast of Southern California lies Catalina Island, a special destination with a personality all its own. For families with more than a few vacation days to spare, Catalina is a different look at what the Southern California coast has to offer.

Although the little island has been inhabited by various nationalities from the past 7,000 years, it was purchased by a family named Banning in the 1880s and turned into the Santa Catalina Island Company. William Wrigley, Jr., of the Chicago gum family, purchased the island in 1919. The island is home to a variety of animals, including buffalo, which were first brought here in the 1920s as "actors" in a movie. Today the wildlife, pristine beaches on the isthmus side, and verdant hills are protected by the Santa Catalina Island Conservancy. No cars are allowed, and hiking and biking outside the main town of Avalon are by permit (free) only.

Kids will find Catalina great for exploring, both on land and in the water. But it is the kind of side trip best enjoyed with children older than 6. No matter what the age of your children, you can make Catalina a day trip or stay the night. The island also affords the opportunity to do some camping. Most every question about what to do in Avalon can be answered on the Green Pleasure Pier (which you'll see when you disembark from the boat) or on the main street.

Catalina is easily reached by boat, especially from Long Beach Harbor. The fastest commute is on the Catalina Express, which runs at least eight round-trips per day (and up to 22 during the busy season), leaving from either Long Beach or San Pedro. Catalina Express also serves both Avalon and Two Harbors; the other cruise lines run less frequent shuttles and serve only Avalon. Round-trip ferry prices from Long Beach or San Pedro are $35 for adults, $26 for kids 2 to 11. (The rate for ferries from Newport Beach or Redondo Beach are slightly higher.) Call the following companies to make reservations and verify departure times and costs:

From Long Beach: Catalina Express (800-464-4228 or 310-519-1212). Approximate travel time: 1 hour.

From San Pedro: Catalina Express (800-464-4228 or 310-519-1212). Approximate travel time: 1 hour, 30 minutes.

From Long Beach: Catalina Adventure Cruises (800-CATA-LINA). Catalina Adventure Cruises leaves only from Long Beach, takes two hours instead of one, and is cheaper (adults $23, kids $19) than Catalina Express. There are far fewer shuttles and thus less choice of times, but many regulars insist that the ride on Catalina Adventure is smoother.

From Newport Beach: Catalina Passenger Service (714-673-5245). Approximate travel time: 1 hour, 15 minutes.

From Redondo Beach: Catalina Express (800-995-4386 or 310-519-1212). Approximate travel time: 1 hour, 45 minutes (summer service only).

A word of caution: The waters can get choppy, and the ride can get bumpy. If anyone in your party is prone to motion sickness, be sure to have medication on hand and consider taking the larger, slower boats of the Catalina Adventure Cruises.

In a rush? You can cut the Long Beach–Avalon commute to a cool 15 minutes if you take the Island Express Helicopter (310-510-2525). Although the helicopter ride is an adventure in its own right, this is a rather pricey way to get to the island—expect to pay about $66 per person one-way, regardless of age.

If you're on a tight touring schedule, it's possible to visit Catalina for the day. Reserve morning and evening passage on the Catalina Express from Long Beach, which runs the most frequent shuttles. If you're staying for only one night, you don't have to bring all your luggage with you. Most families take only a couple of overnight bags with them to Catalina, leaving the bulk of their luggage in the parking lot back in Long Beach. The lot is well lit and guarded, and it beats dragging 14 suitcases behind you for an overnight stay.

If you do decide to stay overnight, you'll find lodging on Catalina to be $85 to $150 per night, with condos costing more. Be sure to make arrangements well in advance for a summer stay-over, especially on weekends when the island is packed. Also note that many hotels require minimum stays during the summer months.

The Santa Catalina Island Company publishes a complete Visitors Guide listing all island hotels and condos and can be obtained by calling the Visitors Bureau at 310-510-1520. If you're pressed for time and don't want to wait for the Visitors Guide, dial 310-510-3000 to reach Catalina Accommodations, which represents a variety of establishments and can handle reservations for everything from a budget motel to a mountainside villa. There are plenty of casual eateries on the island, but be prepared for long waits for a table during prime dining hours.

If you like to camp, Catalina is even cheaper. Cabins and campsites are available for rent through Two Harbors Information (310-510-2800), located on the secluded west end of the island, where you can kayak, snorkel, or fish. If you'd like to be closer to the main harbor and central city of Avalon, try the Hermit Gulch Campground (310-510-TENT). Hermit Gulch is located near the hiking trails and animal preserve within the Wrigley Memorial Garden and is close to tennis, golf, and horseback riding. Rates for both campgrounds are about $8.50 per person per night. In the popular summer camping season, it is essential to make reservations in advance. Spur-of-the-moment decision? At Hermit Gulch, families can rent all their equipment, including tents, tepees, tent cabins, and sleeping bags, starting at $70 for a family of four.

On the Island

One of the best ways to experience the island if you only have a day is to take in one of the terrific tours offered by the Santa Catalina Island Company. Some of the selections are child oriented and painlessly educational. The tours listed here all leave from Avalon and are offered year-round, with the exception of the sea lion and flying fish tours, which are available only in the summer. Call Santa Catalina Discovery Tours (310-510-2500) for a brochure describing the tours in more detail. If you'd like to take more than one tour, some combo deals drop the price. You can plan your time pretty accurately, as each tour duration is listed.

Starlight Undersea Tour

The Starlight is a rare type of boat, a "semisubmersible submarine." It floats on the surface of the water like an ordinary vessel, but beneath the surface hangs an underwater viewing chamber that seats up to 36 people. The Starlight is a great way for kids to have the feel of a sub, and your guides point out the varieties of marine life as you drift through hypnotically waving forests of sea kelp. Kids are given a fish-finder card identifying the species common to these waters, and there's a great race to see who can actually spot the most different kinds of fish. (The guide up on deck periodically throws out bait to ensure you'll see *something*.) On our last trip we got lucky and had a California sea lion follow the boat the whole trip, peering through our windows in bewhiskered bemusement. If you have time for only one tour, make it the Starlight, simply because it's so unusual. The tour lasts 40 minutes and costs $21 for adults, $13 for kids 2 to 11.

Glass Bottom Boat Tours

These tours run both day and night, but the evening tour, which employs underwater lights and often comes upon eels, is especially eerie and fascinating. The fish-finder guide helps make this 40-minute tour not only fun but educational as well. The cost is $8.50 for adults, $4.25 for kids.

Avalon Scenic Tour

Avalon, the principal town on Catalina and America's answer to Monte Carlo, is fairy-tale lovely, especially at night. You see a bit of everything from your bus during this 50-minute tour of the city. The price is $8.50 for adults, $4.25 for kids.

Casino Tour

Don't expect to meet any blackjack dealers—the casino in question is the gorgeous round building you see as you enter the harbor, and its Italian name means simply "gathering place." Built by the Wrigley family in the 1920s, the casino was a prime destination for the wealthy and beautiful who would ferry over to Catalina, then dance all night to the big-band music in the mammoth ballroom. The ballroom, the incredible movie theater, and the views from the circular balconies make this tour worthwhile, although much of the history will be lost on young kids. The tour lasts 50 minutes and costs $8.50 for adults, $4.25 for kids.

Tip: First-run movies still play in the casino theater, so if you're spending the night on Catalina, stroll down and take in a film. You'll never again eat popcorn in such sumptuous surroundings.

Skyline Drive

This two-hour tour takes you into Catalina's interior, where you'll see the infamous buffalo and climb the incredible Skyline Drive by bus to the Airport in the Sky. The Skyline Drive resoundingly proves that there's more to Catalina than Avalon, and the views are unparalleled, making the tour a great favorite with camera buffs. The cost is $17 for adults, $8.50 for kids.

Inland Motor Tour

Taking up where the Skyline Drive Tour leaves off, the Inland Motor Tour goes even deeper into the island's interior, on a search for buffalo, fox, and the bald eagle. You'll also stop and see the Arabian horses at El Rancho Escondido. However, because this tour is four hours long, it's best suited for kids 10 and older. The cost is $29.50 for adults, $14.75 for kids.

Available May Through September Only:
Seal Rocks and the Flying Fish Boat Trip
Seal Rocks is a 55-minute boat ride that takes you to the summer home of the California sea lions. You'll get close enough to observe the seals in their natural habitat—but not too close, as these animals are considerably more vicious than they look. The price is $8.50 for adults, $4.25 for kids.

Another utterly unique experience is the Flying Fish Boat Trip. This evening tour makes use of search lights to illuminate the flying fish that leap from the water and sail through the sky at speeds of 40 miles an hour. The tour lasts 55 minutes, and the cost is $8.50 for adults, $4.25 for kids.

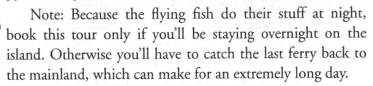

Note: Because the flying fish do their stuff at night, book this tour only if you'll be staying overnight on the island. Otherwise you'll have to catch the last ferry back to the mainland, which can make for an extremely long day.

More Highlights

You don't have to take a tour to see the island. Avalon is small enough to explore by foot, or you can rent a golf cart and drive around the hills and harbors on your own. (The cost is $30 an hour, and you can see a fair amount of the island in that time; if you'd like to keep the golf cart longer, the rate per hour drops.) Unlike a group tour, you can stop whenever something catches your fancy. You can also rent bikes, which are a good way to get around—if you don't plan to ride uphill. There are many sporting opportunities on Catalina: golf, tennis, kayaking, biking, horseback riding, scuba, snorkeling, fishing, and even parasailing. The

Visitors Guide can give you details on the more traditional sports; if you're up for something wilder, call the following:

Kayaking Ocean Sports (310-510-1226) offers kayaking (one-hour rental is $10 for a single, $18 for a double) as well as a kayaking/snorkeling combo, including equipment, kayak, wet suit, and ice chest (half day $31 single, $56 double).

Descanso Beach Sports (310-510-1226), located next to the Casino, offers numerous kayaking adventures, or you can rent a kayak by the hour.

Catalina Divers (800-353-0330 or 310-510-0330). Older kids and strong swimmers may qualify for the two-hour, $85 Intro Dive Package, which includes one hour of instruction, a guided one-hour dive, and all necessary equipment.

Parasailing Catalina (310-510-1777). If you'd rather go above the sea than below, try parasailing. The cost is $40 for a 10-minute parasail ride (although several people go at once, so you'll be on the boat for about an hour). There's no age restriction, but if kids are under 100 pounds, they must fly with an adult.

Catalina Ocean Rafting (310-510-0211) takes you to unexplored parts of the island on these half-day and full-day raft trips. Snorkeling is part of the package. The half-day trip (adults $65, kids $49) is open to kids older than 5. Kids must be at least 12 to tackle the more rugged full-day trip, which costs $130 per person.

If you have more than two days on Catalina, you may want to leave the citified east end of the island, where Avalon lies, and spend some time in the rugged west end, where the chief town is Two Harbors. Campers consider the west end more pristine and outdoorsy, and a wide variety of sporting activities is available, including snorkeling, scuba, ocean kayaking, and safari Jeep tours, which take you deep into the island interior. (Even more remote is Little Harbor, a secluded beach area with ocean trails for camping and hiking.) The Visitors Guide gives details on Two Harbor's lodgings and activities, and transport between Avalon and Two Harbors can be arranged by calling Catalina Express (800-995-4386 or 310-519-1212) or Two Harbors directly (310-510-2800).

No matter which side of the island you visit or how long you decide to stay, the trip to Catalina Island is bound to be memorable. One family who made a day trip reported that they had time to take in three tours, explore the beaches and shops of Avalon, go cruising in a golf cart, have dinner at a seafood restaurant by the pier, and still catch the ferry back to the mainland. Making the plans necessary to get to the island may seem like a hassle now, but along with Hollywood and Beverly Hills, Catalina Island ranks as a quintessentially Southern California experience.

WHALE-WATCHING AND HARBOR TOURS

Some of the piers offer daily harbor cruises year-round. Most kids enjoy spending an hour on a boat exploring the rocky Pacific coast, and it's a low-stress, low-cost way to see the shore. If you're at a beach with a pier, look for a cruise line booth; reservations are often not necessary. Spirit Cruises (562-495-5884), which leaves from the busy but conveniently located Long Beach Harbor, offers 75-minute harbor cruises (adults $9, kids $5).

Whale-watching is a much bigger deal. December through April is the migration season for the gray whales, which annually travel in pods from the Bering Sea to the warm waters off Baja, California. Whale-watching is very popular with locals, so reservations are a must. (If you want to take a weekend cruise, make reservations before you leave home.) Prices are $15 for adults, $8 for kids; the cruises last from two to three hours. The major cruise lines employ helicopter surveillance to direct the boats and make it more likely to see whales; many lines offer guaranteed sightings, or the second trip is free. Whale-watching is a special treat but probably should be reserved for kids 7 and older. Younger children may grow restless on the boat, and the windy, slippery decks require parents to keep a tight grip on toddlers and preschoolers. Whale-watching can get damp, so bring a waterproof jacket even in the summer and wear skid-resistant footwear. And although the boats are well stabilized, some people do experience motion sickness. There are over-the-counter medications to help control the dizziness and nausea; if boats get to you, begin taking the medication 24 hours before you plan to board. For information on times and prices, call Catalina Cruises (800-CATALINA), Spirit Cruises (562-495-5884), or Star Party Cruises (562-431-6833).

GRIFFITH PARK

Griffith Park in Los Angeles sprawls over 4,000 acres in the eastern part of the Santa Monica Mountains. Families with a week in the L.A. area should make a day of visiting the park, which houses the Los Angeles Zoo, the Autry Museum of Western Heritage, the Griffith Observatory and Laserium, the Travel Town Museum, pony rides, and lots of picnic areas.

Los Angeles Zoo

The Los Angeles Zoo is divided into areas that correspond to the five continents, and you may feel like you're literally going around the world during your touring. You'll definitely need a map and a stroller. The Safari Shuttle (adults $3, kids $1), which makes several stops around the zoo grounds, helps cut down on the walking. If your kids are young or your time is limited, focus on a single segment— African animals, for example. The Adventure Island children's section, featuring animals of the American Southwest, contains many interactive exhibits and is especially neat for young kids who enjoy pressing a button and hearing a mountain lion roar. The shows are also worthwhile—the zookeepers are full of fun facts about the animals and happy to answer questions. Animals and You is the best show for younger kids; if your kids are younger than 7, drop by the small children's zoo, which has a nursery for baby animals and their mothers. The Los Angeles Zoo is open daily (except Christmas) from 10 A.M. to 5 P.M.; admission is $8.25 for adults, $3.25 for kids, and discount coupons are easy to find. For more information about the zoo, call 213-666-4090.

Autry Museum of Western Heritage

The Autry Museum is a definite must if you're in the park. This museum is devoted to acquiring, preserving, and interpreting art and artifacts related to the history of the West. In addition to the usual behind-the-glass exhibitions, youngsters will enjoy The Los Angeles Times Children's Discovery Gallery, where they can follow the life of a Mexican American family in Arizona over 170 years, beginning in the 1800s. They can dress up in period clothing and examine journals. But don't end your visit there. On the same floor, kids get a kick out of riding a stationary horse while a video camera places them in a scene from "The Lone Ranger." Learn about how cowboys, Native Americans, and women have been portrayed in westerns over the years. Downstairs, all of you can travel through the history of the West—learn about a cowboy's life on the range, view an authentic antique stagecoach and saloon bar, and watch a re-creation of the "Shoot-Out at OK Corral." Be sure to ask about special children's programs often offered in summer.

There's a café, and strollers are available. The museum is in the park at the junction of the Golden State (I-5) and the Ventura (I-134) freeways, not far from the zoo. Admission is $7.50 for adults, $5 for kids 13 to 18, $3 for kids 2 to 12. For hours, call 213-667-2000.

Griffith Observatory and Laserium

Budding astronomers will enjoy an afternoon at the Griffith Observatory, which happens to be the largest astronomy museum in the western United States. Each day, two shows at the Planetarium introduce kids to the wonders of the universe. If your children are under 5, take them to the special 1:30 P.M. weekend shows. Atop the Observatory you'll get a good chance for clear summer nights when the Zeiss telescope is open. If there are preteens or teens in your group, they'll enjoy the evening Laserium laser-light concerts. Show times are 6 P.M. and 8:45 P.M. On Friday and Saturday there's a 9:45 P.M. show. The best part of visiting the Observatory? It's free. Call 213-664-1191 for general information and 818-901-9405 for Laserium concert details.

There are other activities in Griffith Park especially suited to kids under 7. At Travel Town Museum, they can play railroad engineer and climb aboard the full-size locomotives. The museum is open daily and is located in the northwest corner of the park.

At the Los Feliz Boulevard entrance, you can line up for pony and stagecoach rides for a nominal fee. These take place Tuesday through Sunday. Not far from the ponies is the Merry-Go-Round, which—for you carousel fans—was built in 1926. You can ride daily in summer and the rest of the year on weekends only.

Griffith Park has plenty of parking, several food stands, 53 miles of hiking trails, and picnic areas (some with barbecue grills and nearby restrooms).

As in any big-city park, you should exercise caution by staying in the heavily trafficked areas, and you should be on your way by dusk.

MUSEUMS

Los Angeles has some wonderful museums. They can be a fun—and educational—option.

The J. Paul Getty Museum

1200 Getty Center Drive, Brentwood

310-440-7300

The new, gorgeous, $1 billion Getty Museum opened to amazing fanfare just before this book went to press. Although advance reservations must be made for parking in the 1,500-car lot, thousands of people swarmed the Center in its opening weeks by parking in nearby residential areas and hiking up to the museum, forcing the Getty to take out ads in the newspapers asking people to hold off visiting until after the holidays. By the time you read this, things should have calmed down a bit. But it is still advisable to call for a reservation as soon as you know the dates of your visit to Los Angeles.

The Getty, originally located in a beautiful villa in Malibu, is now spread over 110 acres on a hilltop in Brentwood. On display are its rare permanent collections of Renaissance manuscripts; pre-twentieth-century European paintings by masters such as Goya, Michelangelo, Rembrandt, and Monet; and sculpture, decorative arts, photography, and temporary exhibits. Its art collection is possibly unsurpassed in the world. But if this sounds too stuffy for your kids, think again. The Getty has gone all out for families, bringing in cutting-edge interactive and participatory activities. Game Boxes, such as those first conceived at the original Getty, give kids an opportunity to explore pretty much on their own. By having to solve the mysteries of complex paintings, kids get a chance to view art on their own terms. A special pamphlet, "Going to the Getty," was written to guide the kids through the Center, and there are myriad special events scheduled for all age-groups, featuring storytelling, family festivals, and other activities. A special Family Room geared toward kids 5 to 13 is stocked with CD-ROMs, and there are specialists staffing the room to answer questions. Strollers are allowed throughout the museum.

In addition to the galleries, the Getty Center has gorgeous gardens, a fine restaurant, an indoor and outdoor cafeteria, and a snack center at the tram.

To visit the museum by car, you must make a reservation by calling the phone number listed above (available 24 hours a day). Although admission to the museum is free, there's a $5 charge for parking. If you don't want to drive, you can arrive by bus, taxi, motorcycle, or bicycle without a reservation. If you decide to arrive by car without a reservation, be forewarned that parking in the nearby residential areas is severely restricted. The Getty is right off the San Diego Freeway (I-405) at Getty Center Drive. Metro Bus #561 or Santa Monica Big Blue Bus #14 stops at the entrance. Once you get there, a four-and-a-half-minute tram ride will get you to the entrance. The Getty is open Saturday and Sunday 10 A.M. to 6 P.M., Tuesday and Wednesday 11 A.M. to 7 P.M., and Thursday and Friday to 9 P.M.

Natural History Museum

900 Exposition Boulevard, downtown Los Angeles
213-763-3466

Although they're not located in the same place, the Natural History Museum is part of a family of museums that includes the La Brea Tar Pits and the Peterson Automotive Museum. The Natural History Museum is in beautiful Exposition Park near downtown Los Angeles and is near the IMAX Theater and the new Science Museum. If you plan to visit all three, be sure to allow a full day.

As the museum is so big and your time may be limited, pick the highlights to visit with the kids. Many children want to visit the dinosaur exhibits first. Next take them to the popular Schreiber Hall of Birds with its three walk-though habitats, animated birds, and learning stations. Finally, be sure to visit the Ralph M. Parsons Discovery Center and Insect Zoo, tucked away near the Rotunda. This is an especially good choice for a rainy day or when the kids are tired of walking. Here they finally get to touch and explore. Some youngsters make fossil rubbings, while others touch the stuffed lion and bear and examine their pelts. Interactive Discovery boxes, full of educational activities having to do with nature, can be checked out over and over again. Upstairs is the Insect Zoo, not my favorite place, but deliciously exciting to the children. There's a giant ant farm that you'll be glad is there rather than at home, creepy tarantulas and scorpions, busy beetles, and a stocked refrigerator of insect delicacies!

If you have more time to spend in the summer, check out the museum's educational or family programs. Sometimes there are overnights focusing on a particular exhibit, weeklong science camps, and many special events. Admission is $6 for adults, $3.50 for teens 13 to 18, $2 for kids 5 to 12. Parking is $5. Closed Monday. Call for hours.

A short walk past the beautiful rose garden will take you to Los Angeles's new California Science Center (due to open after this book goes to press), and nearby is the IMAX Theater.

La Brea Tar Pits

5801 Wilshire Boulevard, Los Angeles
213-934-PAGE

Although its real name is the George C. Page Museum of La Brea Discoveries, most people know it as the La Brea Tar Pits. This area, formerly a Mexican land grant, was once mined for its sticky black asphalt. As they dug, miners came upon one of the world's most abundant fossil sites. Your family will get to see the remains of giant ground sloths, saber-toothed cats, dire wolves, and many of the little insects that got stuck in the gooey liquid that we call tar.

Over thousands of years, millions of animals were trapped by the ooze and their remains preserved by asphalt. That's why the paleontologists here have discovered more than three million fossils, many of animals now extinct.

You can bring the kids and spend one or two hours. In addition to the exhibits, they'll get to see the actual glass-enclosed Paleontology Laboratory, where the newly discovered bones are cleaned and identified—yes, newly discovered. Digging is still going on at the museum. In fact, if you're in Los Angeles in the summer, call to find out if Pit 91 is open. Visitors can watch as the museum's paleontologists and volunteers unearth fossils 10,000 to 40,000 years old. It's free to watch and usually open Wednesday through Sunday during certain summer months.

Admission to the museum is $6 for adults, $3.50 for teens, $2 for kids under 12. Parking is $5 with a validation. Closed Monday.

Peterson Automotive Museum

6060 Wilshire Boulevard, Los Angeles
213-930-CARS

What could be more Los Angeles than a museum devoted to displaying the automobile? More than 200 cars, trucks, and motorcycles are displayed in this huge building, and their influence on our culture is easy to comprehend.

A special treat is the museum's new Discovery Center, spread out on the third floor. Although the interactive exhibits are geared toward kids 6 to 16, there is a special corner for toddlers, complete with a stroller parking area. Parents can entertain them with children's books while their siblings take off to experience the "stations." One nice thing about this: The kids will be getting an education while having fun!

The idea here is to learn basic scientific principles using cars and car parts as the teaching tools. There are three sections to the Discovery Center. The VroomRoom is a cacophony of sounds. There are alarms and engines and sirens and all sorts of noises that illustrate how sound and light change on the basis of motion—the Doppler effect.

The East Wing houses, in addition to the toddler area, the side of a Sparkletts Water truck. Each insert that would have held bottled water on an actual truck now holds a water bottle filled with a different learning experience. For example, kids check out a "bottle" of gears and can practice putting them together. Another holds design elements of automobiles, and yet another holds sample parts of a car to teach what a car is made of. A child-proofed 1910 Model T is available for exploring. Another highlight is the Driver's Education automobile simulator—a must for any preteen or teen in your family. A highly sophisticated software program replicates real-time driving situations—your child will experience what it's like driving the freeways, encountering emergency vehicles, or suffering through congested traffic.

The West Wing is where kids in fourth grade and beyond will spend most of their time. A variety of hands-on exhibits let them experiment with traction and friction, viscosity, centrifugal force, gravity, momentum, and other scientific properties. But don't tell them how educational it is. Tell them there are more than a dozen stations they can touch and move, and create their own experiments, including a giant engine and pistons where they can become a human spark plug.

The Peterson is open Tuesday through Sunday from 10 A.M. to 6 P.M. Tickets cost $7 for adults, $3 for kids 5 to 12. Parking is $4.

Museum of Flying

> 2772 Donald Douglas Loop North (Santa Monica Airport), Santa Monica
> 310-392-8822 for hours and directions

Although not exactly near any major sightseeing venues, the Museum of Flying in Santa Monica may appeal to the nascent pilots in your family. This is an especially good diversion on one of those rare rainy days in Los Angeles or when the afternoon turns hot and smoggy. The three-level museum is located adjacent to the north runway of the Santa Monica Airport, not far from where Douglas Aircraft Company was founded in the 1920s.

In addition to the museum's large collection of World War II fighter planes, there's the world's smallest jet, which was featured in a James Bond movie. The children's area— Airventure—is especially appropriate for grade-school children. They can participate in model building, climb into real cockpits, ride in the simulator, and join scheduled workshops. Call the museum for hours and workshop information. Also ask them about their dining program with the adjacent DC3 Restaurant Tuesday through Friday evenings. For one set price and menu, parents get a quiet dinner out while the kids eat and are supervised at the museum.

Museum admission is $7 for adults, $3 for kids. Closed Monday.

Los Angeles Children's Museum

310 North Main Street, Los Angeles
213-687-8800 for information and directions

Located downtown in the L.A. Mall, the Children's Museum is designed for kids younger than 10, with many activities slanted toward toddlers and preschoolers. The emphasis is on interactive exhibits—kids can pretend to be an anchorwoman on the evening news, explore a dinosaur cave, dress up in fireman's gear, "drive" a bus, and build a castle with giant Velcro blocks. Arts-and-crafts activities change monthly and revolve around specific themes. In addition to workshops, storytellers, musicians, actors, and other presenters appear in the museum's theater. We've spent many hours in the Recycle Art Studio making elaborate creations from boxes of recycled materials.

Admission is $5, regardless of age, and there is nearby parking in the L.A. Mall garage. The museum is open year-round, Saturday and Sunday from 10 A.M. to 5 P.M. From late June to early September it's also open weekdays from 11:30 A.M. to 5 P.M.

TELEVISION, MOVIES, AND RADIO

A trip to California wouldn't be complete without taking a tour of a studio or learning the history of the entertainment industry.

Television Studio Tours

The sets of most of the TV series filmed in Los Angeles are closed to anyone under 16, so don't casually promise the kids they'll be able to see a taping of their favorite show. Some Fox and Nickelodeon shows let in younger kids;

"Saved by the Bell" allows kids as young as 12. Each studio has a different policy regarding children at tapings, and a studio may even have different policies for different shows, so check before you leave home.

The NBC studio tour, however, welcomes kids. This tour allows you to visit TV show sets and learn a bit about special effects, wardrobe, makeup, and set construction. It usually lasts one to one-and-a-half hours. The cost is $7 for adults, $3.75 for kids younger than 12. For details, call 818-840-3537. The NBC tour is a good alternative for families who are not planning to visit Universal Studios.

Paramount Studios (213-956-5575) offers a two-hour walking tour on weekdays. Children must be 10 or over. The tour is $15, and you must reserve in advance. Warner Brothers (818-954-1744) also offers a studio tour, but it's quite technical and more expensive. The two-hour tour is open to kids over 10, and the cost is $30. Reserve in advance. Weekdays only.

To learn which shows are taping during your stay, whether any game shows are auditioning contestants, and how to get tickets, call the numbers below.

ABC (handled by Audiences Unlimited)	818-753-3470
CBS Television City	213-852-2624
NBC	818-840-3537
Fox (handled by Audiences Unlimited)	818-753-3470

If you'd like to be part of the audience during the taping of a show, there are three ways to get free tickets: (1) Pick them up in person on the day of taping, either at the studio itself or at the ticket kiosks located on Universal's CityWalk near Universal Studios. If you choose to wait until the day of taping, tickets for the most popular shows are unlikely to be available. (2) Stop by the Audiences Unlimited ticket booth while touring Universal Studios and see who's filming the next day. They handle tickets from several different studios, so the selection is a little better, but remember that the most popular shows may be gone. There are also studio booths in Hollywood offering next-day tickets. (3) Write for tickets in advance. This is your best bet if you want to see a popular series. Confirm what will be filming during your stay by phone, get the studio address, and then send a written ticket request along with a stamped self-addressed envelope.

Note: Even a ticket doesn't guarantee you'll get in. To ensure a seat, line up an hour before the stated time on the ticket. Hollywood Group Services can guarantee seating, but reservations must be made with a credit card, and if you don't show up, you're charged $10. Call them at 310-914-3400. Paramount Studios will also reserve seats at 213-956-5575.

Once you get tickets, you'll devote a sizable chunk of a day to the taping—and because young kids aren't allowed, you may have to find a sitter during the day, which can be tricky. In short, seeing a taping is tough on families with young kids. It may be better to visit Universal Studios or take the NBC tour and save a taping for your next trip to California.

The Museum of Television and Radio

465 North Beverly Drive, Beverly Hills
310-786-1000

This museum, interesting to kids over 10, is for TV aficionados and those who appreciate the drama and humor of radio. State-of-the-art equipment allows you to find and access more than 90,000 TV and radio programs covering the past 75 years. There are family viewing stations at which you can tap into these resources. If you visit in late fall, you can attend screenings of the films entered in the Annual International Children's Television Festival.

But possibly the best reason to visit with the kids is the Radio Workshop series. Radio drama is an art that many children—and parents—aren't aware of. Children ages 9 to 14 read scripts and operate sound effects from some of the best-known shows in the history of radio, such as "The Shadow" and "Superman." Each performance is watched by an audience and is recorded, and an audiocassette is mailed to the child. Dates for these workshops change quarterly, and you must sign up and pay in advance. There's an extra $5 charge per adult or child. The tape is free. For reservations, call 310-786-1014. Admission to the museum is $6 for adults and kids. Hours are limited, so call ahead.

WHERE TO STAY IN LOS ANGELES

It is almost impossible to find a hotel room for under $125 in Los Angeles. However, travel clubs, corporate and AAA discounts, or off-season travel may help. Always ask for other rates—don't accept the first one offered.

Loews Santa Monica

> 1700 Ocean Avenue, Santa Monica
> 800-23-LOEWS or 310-458-6700

Loews has a great beachfront location—rare in Los Angeles—and you can still reach all the other area sights easily. The pool is wonderful and the beach only a stroll away. While the children are in the Splash Club, you can opt for a few hours at the full-service spa.

Loews children's program, the Splash Club, is for kids 5 to 12. The morning and afternoon session ($35 per session) include beach and pool games and arts and crafts. The Splash Club runs daily in the summer; in the off-season planned activities for children can be arranged, but you must make reservations 24 hours in advance with the concierge.

Rooms begin at $240, but there are numerous packages. Even if Loews is out of your price range, consider stopping by for the stellar Sunday brunch. The brunch is a visual and culinary feast and qualifies as a minisplurge for the family who has hit one drive-thru too many. The price is $35 for adults; kids are charged $12 and have their own buffet table.

Sheraton Universal

333 Universal Terrace Parkway, Universal City,
    Hollywood
800-325-3535 or 818-980-1212

This hotel may have the best location in all of Los Angeles. You're minutes from downtown, Hollywood, and Beverly Hills, and shuttles run continually between the hotel and Universal Studios/CityWalk, meaning you can go for days without moving your car. In short, you're close to big-city action without a big-city feel.

If you opt to stay here, you can get discounted rates for Universal Studios. There's a good selection of restaurants and amenities, and because production crews filming at Universal often stay here, you may even spot a star in the lobby or by the pool. The staff is attentive, and families are made to feel welcome. But the three chief advantages to the Sheraton Universal are location, location, and location.

Consider making it home base during the Hollywood–Beverly Hills–central L.A. segment of your trip.

Regular rates begin at about $250, but there are numerous packages that include some Universal Studios tickets and self-parking. If you reserve seven days in advance—and if these rooms are available—your rate could go down to $165 *and* include breakfast for two. It's pretty unlikely for this to happen in summer, but be sure to inquire about all the options. Call the hotel directly.

Holiday Inn Select

1150 South Beverly Drive, Beverly Hills
800-HOLIDAY or 310-553-6561

This high-rise hotel is centrally located and has a heated pool and a restaurant. Rooms are comfortable and serviceable. In summer, rack rates are $165. But there are a variety of discounts that apply, depending on occupancy, that can bring the price to $140. Be sure to inquire about special rates.

Hotel Shangri-La

1301 Ocean Avenue, Santa Monica
800-STAY or 310-394-2791

This funky hotel, well placed near the Third Street Promenade and the Santa Monica Pier, has one-bedroom suites with full kitchens starting at $160. There are several room configurations, so be sure to tell them your needs.

Travelodge Los Angeles West

10740 Santa Monica Boulevard, Westwood
800-255-3050 or 310-474-4576

Families on a budget should take a peak at this little spot. Rooms are quite affordable—about $75 for a room with two queen-size beds, and the location is great.

WHERE TO EAT IN LOS ANGELES

• Hard Rock Café (310-276-7605) is located in the Beverly Center shopping mall in West Hollywood. It's a must-stop for anyone older than 9, but younger kids love it as well. After a tour of Hollywood or Beverly Hills, this is a good stop. But be sure to come early. From 6 P.M. on, the lines grow long, and the music gets louder and louder as the night goes on. Kids will be entranced by the Cadillac perched on top of the entrance, the chance to make Elton John's electric eyeglasses light up, and the various motorcycles, guitars, and autographed memorabilia on display; adults will be pleasantly surprised by the fast, friendly service and not-too-outrageous prices. If you want only to purchase a T-shirt or jacket with the famous Hard Rock logo, be aware that the line to buy merchandise is separate from the restaurant line—be sure you're in the right one. If you want to both eat and shop, ask your server to bring your souvenir selections directly to the table and add them to the food bill. That way you'll avoid having to get into two different lines and paying twice. There's also a location at Universal's CityWalk.

• Planet Hollywood (310-275-7828), in the heart of Beverly Hills, is to the movies what Hard Rock is to music: a cool choice for California cuisine, nonstop entertainment, and great souvenirs. There's also a line for this restaurant, so arrive early.

- Dive (310-788-3483) is Steven Spielberg's funky submarine-themed restaurant serving—what else?—submarine sandwiches. You'll find it in the Century City Shopping Center.

- Tony Roma's (310-659-7427) is *the* place to go for ribs. There's one located on L.A.'s Restaurant Row (La Cienega Boulevard) in Beverly Hills.

- Ed Debevic's (310-659-1952) is a '50s-style diner complete with dancing/singing waitpersons who aren't too shy to boogie with your kids. It is nearby Tony Roma's and especially fun for kids.

- Johnny Rockets (310-271-2222) is a smaller '50s-style diner serving a more limited menu of chili fries, burgers, and malts. But the prices are great, and you can sit at the counter. There are several locations, including one in Beverly Hills.

- The Cheesecake Factory (310-278-7270) in Beverly Hills offers 36 different kinds of killer cheesecake and an excellent Sunday brunch. But it's always crowded, so try to come between prime dining hours.

CHAPTER *10*

Side Trippin' to San Diego

San Diego is a vacation destination in itself. You could travel to California and visit only San Diego and the surrounding area and spend two weeks doing it. But if your destination is Los Angeles or Anaheim and you have longer than a week available, consider a side trip to San Diego for two or three days.

San Diego, the site of the first European settlement in California, is also a city of harbor excursions, a magnificent urban park, a world-renown zoo, and beautiful beaches. The city is a straight two-and-a-half-hour drive down I-5 from Los Angeles and is about an hour and a half from Anaheim. Although it is possible to zip down for the day, you really need to stay overnight to fully appreciate the city. (See the end of this chapter for information about accommodations.)

There is lots to do in San Diego. Following is a description of some of the best choices.

WATER SPORTS AND WHALE-WATCHING

There are plenty of opportunities for water sports around San Diego. You can rent sailboats and windsurfers at the Mission Bay Sports Center (619-488-1004). From December to March, San Diego is center stage to some of the best whale-watching in all of California. But you'll be fighting the locals for space on the boats, so make reservations before you leave home. San Diego Harbor Excursions, at the Embarcadero, offers one-hour coastal cruises year-round. The cost is $12 for adults, $6 for kids 4 to 12, plus whale-watching. The other outfits listed below schedule fishing and sailing expeditions, and some offer whale-watching tours as well; call a couple of days in advance to book a coastal cruise or fishing tour.

San Diego Harbor Excursions	619-234-4111
Fisherman's Landing	619-222-0391
H and M Landing	619-222-1144
Point Loma Sportfishing	619-223-1627

OLD TOWN

San Diego State Historic Park
(From I-5, exit Old Town Avenue)

In addition to the other attractions that follow, take a few hours to visit Old Town, where San Diego was born. Old Town is an important historic area, and there's a collection of shops and restaurants that preserve the flavor of the settlers. Mixed with the new are numerous original buildings, including the oldest adobe building, dating from 1827. If you're short on time, pick up a map at the Old Town Information Center (619-220-5422) and take a self-guided walking tour.

Tours

These are tours even your youngsters will enjoy. The Old Town Trolley (619-298-8687) will take you on a two-hour guided tour. But rather than sitting through an entire tour all at once, you can get on and off at nine different locations, including Coronado. Pick it up in Old Town. The cost is $20 for adults, $8 for kids under 12. For a different kind of tour, you can hop on a horse-drawn carriage supplied by Cinderella Carriages, located at Seaport Village near the Harbor House Restaurant.

BALBOA PARK

Adjacent to the San Diego Zoo
619-239-0512 for directions and hours

Balboa Park just may be one of the country's most beautiful urban parks. We never get tired of exploring the grounds and visiting the museums. The ornate Spanish Colonial Revival buildings were originally built for the 1915–16 Panama-California Exposition. Today many of them are venues for the museums and cultural centers in the park. Balboa Park is also home to the famous Old Globe Theatre (try to catch a performance when you're in town) and the San Diego Zoo.

If you plan to spend much time visiting the museums, buy a Passport to Balboa Park, which admits you to 11 of the 14 museums for $19 (a $56 value) and is valid for a week. Pick one up at the Visitors Center or any of the participating museums in the park.

In addition to strolling through the grounds and catching a mime or a balloon maker—or perhaps a reggae group—in Plaza del Balboa, families can pick from a wealth of activities. Youngsters will want to visit the Marie Hitchcock Puppet Theater, and train buffs will opt for seeing the San Diego Model Railroad Museum, which exhibits the largest permanent operating scale model and toy train display in the United States. The Automotive Museum and the Aerospace Museum are also interesting. Sports fans will like the San Diego Hall of Champions—16,000 square feet of sports museum. Be sure to take the children to see the Oaxacan weaver and the Mexican tortilla maker at the Museum of Man. By the time you read this, the Reuben H. Fleet Space Theater and Science Center should be ready with its Simulation Technology Center, which will take you to the Earth's center and even inside the human body. There's lots more to do and see. Stop by the Visitors Center for a list of museums and daily activities. For little children who need to work off some energy (and have been sitting quietly in their strollers), head for the children's area near the zoo, where they can ride "butterfly rides," a carousel, and a miniature train. Most, but not all, of the museums are open daily.

BEACHES

Some of the most beautiful beaches in California can be found in San Diego. La Jolla Cove is one of these. Nearby Children's Pool Beach, which is protected by a concrete breakwater, is great if you have little kids in tow. Mission Bay Park, the manmade aquatic area, is popular for families because the waters are so calm, there's plenty of parking, and picnic tables are abundant. Families can also ride bikes or roller-skate. Coronado Beach is long and quiet, and its sand is bleached white. At Mission Beach there's a great old wooden roller coaster.

SEA WORLD

Sea World is a low-stress, low-tech park that can easily be seen in a day. Children will learn something new no matter how many times they visit.

Details

1720 South Shores Road, Mission Bay, San Diego
714-939-6212 from Los Angeles and Orange
County; 619-226-3901 in San Diego

Sea World is located just off I-5 about 90 minutes south of Anaheim and two hours from Los Angeles. The park is open daily from 9 A.M. to dusk, with extended evening hours in the summer and during major holidays. Admission is $29 for adults, $21 for kids 3 to 11; it's easy to either find discount coupons in area magazines or buy discounted tickets through area hotels. For seasonal hours of operation and directions, call the park.

Highlights

To your kids, Sea World is probably best known as the home of Shamu and the killer whales. But the park is divided into several categories: animal interaction, exhibits, aquariums, shows, and what they call "adventures."

New and returning visitors flock to Rocky Point Preserve to feed and pet the "smiling" dolphins. Your kids will get the chance to pet the fierce-looking-but-really-gentle bat rays at Forbidden Reef and feed the cute-but-really-fierce sea lions at their own pool. The Shark Encounter is a definite must. Visitors move through a tunnel-like area surrounded by thick glass. Behind that glass swim sharks of almost all descriptions.

The California Tidepools is one of the most popular spots to introduce your young children to the wonders that live in the sea. Park animal-care experts show the kids how to properly handle a starfish and touch a sea urchin, and they teach them about sea anemones. This is one of our favorite spots, and we return to it year after year, each time learning something new.

The exhibits aren't at all boring, especially the Penguin Encounter, where the tuxedoed birds strut their stuff behind big glass walls. Many a time we've been able to watch the trainers feed and interact with the noble birds, and it's a lot of fun. Your daily information sheet and map list feeding times.

There are few shows, but they're all quite good, especially the Sea Lion and Otter Show, where the antics of sea lions Clyde and Seamore are still as funny as the first time we saw them.

The newest adventure at Sea World is Wild Arctic, a simulated helicopter ride to a base station in the frozen Arctic. This one received mixed feedback. There are two ways to experience this attraction: You can line up for the motion jet helicopter or, if you're prone to motion sickness, take the gyrostabilized ride. I opted for the nonmotion helicopter. The simulation takes you over the Arctic; as you "fly over," you escape an avalanche, and your copter drops off a breaking glacier. The nonmotion experience was pretty boring. The rest of the family took the motion ride and said it was pretty rough. But happily it lasted only a few minutes. Remember that this is an adventure, not a ride.

Once you "land" at the re-created base, proceed through the mythic research base on foot and watch beluga whales and walruses at play in a natural-like habitat, complete with the "remains" of a wrecked exploration ship. There are all sorts of scientific displays, monitors, a sonograph reading out the whale vocalizations, touch screens to plan your own exploration, and research equipment that the professional scientists would use.

This attraction is fine for any age (there's a 42-inch height requirement)—just decide whether your child can handle the motion simulator. If they survived Back to the Future, they'll have no problem with Wild Arctic.

The Extras

Visitors can sign up for "Dine with Shamu" and eat lunch at a tankside table in Shamu Stadium. The killer whales play in the tank, and the trainers visit with the guests to answer questions. It's quite clever but expensive.

Sign up for this immediately upon entering the park, as it fills up rapidly. So as not to disappoint the kids, who may be counting on this, call ahead. It's available only on weekends and certain weekdays. The cost of the lunch is $24.95 for adults, $12.95 for kids. Reservations can be made by calling 619-226-3601.

The Behind-the-Scenes Tour is a good one for families who plan to spend the day and evening at Sea World. It is best appreciated by children 7 and older or by parents with sleeping infants. Younger kids may get bored halfway through. Taking the tour assures you of a reserved seat at the Shamu show.

During the 90-minute walking tour, we saw the Animal Care Facility, where beached, ill, or retired animals are cared for. Everyone was fascinated to learn just how much fish is needed for the mammals in the park. Shamu's friends alone consume 150 to 250 pounds of fish a day!

As you continue past the animal ER unit, to the Underwater Classroom, and finally to Shamu's stadium between shows, youthful, friendly guides share all sorts of educational tidbits, from how the water gets filtered in the tanks (once you see the size of Shamu's tanks, you'll be amazed to learn the water can be filtered in three minutes) to the difference between fins and flippers and what makes an adult flamingo pink. The 9- and 10-year-olds on our tour loved to ask questions. Ardavan, a 9-year-old boy from Los Angeles, reported he had taken the tour a couple of times and never found it boring. The tours are not always the same. The guides choose the sites on the basis of time and availability. Sign up for the tour when you arrive at the park. The cost is $6 for adults, $5 for kids.

Shamu's Happy Harbor, a good stop in middle of the day when the youngsters need a break, is a creative play area where kids can explore water mazes and climb through tunnels, up realistic rigging, and over bridges. (A separate toddler section allows younger kids to play among balls or bounce on an air mattress with no danger of being trampled by 8-year-olds.) Shamu's Happy Harbor has been expanded and revamped into one of the most inviting play areas in Southern California. In addition, there's an arcade full of midway style games, a gondola-car sky ride over Mission Bay Park and Skytower ($2 each or $3 for both), and the Budweiser clydesdales.

Touring Tips

• Several times during the day, kids are allowed to feed the sea lions or dolphins, and spending $2 for a few fish to toss is well worth it (but remember those sea gulls circling overhead just waiting to grab one out of your hand). The dolphin tanks are designed so that kids can actually lean over and touch one as they glide past; the exhibits don't rush you and offer your best chance to really observe the animals.

• If you want to take the Behind-the-Scenes tour, sign up first thing in the morning. (The tour booth is just to the right after you enter.) The price is reasonable, the guides are knowledgeable and patient with kids, the groups are held to 25 people or fewer, and a bonus perk is a reserved seat for the popular Shamu show.

Even if you don't think your kids are up to a 90-minute tour (or if they're really interested in only one animal), try to talk to one of the trainers. After the shows, trainers make themselves available for questions.

• Showing up at feeding time (also marked on your map) can likewise be a learning experience.

• At the Forbidden Reef, don't miss the underwater viewing area, where dozens of eels and skates will give you the willies.

• Eat inside the stadiums if you're pressed for time. Sea World's Shamu kids' meal is easy to transport and guaranteed to please youngsters raised on drive-thru cuisine.

• In recognition of the fact that Dads also travel with kids, Sea World has gender-neutral changing stations between the men's and women's restrooms.

• Sea World has a large selection of marine-themed stuffed animals, such as an adorable plush Shamu, and they're cheaper here than at most zoos and theme parks.

• The dolphin-shaped strollers, available as you enter the park, are so nifty that most kids climb in without a fuss. Because the stadiums are located rather far apart, strollers are a good idea for preschoolers.

• The first eight rows of the stadiums are earmarked as the "splash zone," and they're not kidding. Anyone sitting too close will get drenched, especially at the Shamu show. Those killer whales can leap high—and upon reentry, they don't exactly cut the water like a knife. (Shamu's Happy Harbor also has lots of water games that will leave young kids dripping wet.) If you're touring in the winter or spring, when it can get chilly, bring a change of T-shirts for the kids and let them start the day in a lightweight jacket. There are lockers located near the tour sign-up desk.

• A Mother's Nursing Room can be found near the Beached Animals Exhibit.

Touring Plan

1. Arrive at the park about 20 minutes before the stated opening time. After you get tickets and maps, you'll be allowed into a courtyard where you can have a muffin from the bakery, browse the shops, and be ready for the walk to Wild Arctic.

2. The show times will determine your schedule. One of the best helps is the daily program, which gives times of the shows and feeding schedules. There are five major shows at Sea World. See two or three in the morning while the kids are still fresh, then take a break. The suggested show schedule printed on your map is a good one, designed to cut backtracking and keep wait times to a minimum. If you have young kids who don't have the stamina to see every show, simply skip one in the middle of the day, let them hang out a while in the play area, and then resume the schedule.

    Shamu is the most crowded show, and you'll need to be there 20 to 30 minutes early to assure a good seat. The Pilot Whale and Dolphin Show and the Sea Lion and Otter Show are the next most popular, but the stadiums are large, so being there 15 minutes early will suffice. The Bird Show, the film *Window to the Sea,* and water-ski show are less crowded; show up about 10 minutes before show time. All the stadium shows have clever preshows to make the wait time go fast—the mime at the Sea Lion and Otter Show is hilarious.

3. Work in continuous exhibits, such as the Shark Encounter or Penguin Encounter, at your leisure.

4. After you've seen several shows, take a break; in summer, when the park is open until 9 P.M., you might opt to return to your hotel, but you probably won't need to. Several families mentioned picnicking at nearby Mission Bay Park or within Sea World's own picnic grounds. If you plan to stay within Sea World, the small deli inside the Anheuser-Busch Hospitality Center is cheerily attractive and generally less crowded than other food stands around the park. (Adults can have two free beer samples.) Midafternoon is also a good time to visit Shamu's Happy Harbor or take the Skyride or Skytower. And just after lunch is a great time to take the guided tour.

5. Return to see two or three more shows. In summer, hang around for the final Shamu Show of the night.

SAN DIEGO ZOO

Families accustomed to their hometown zoo, which they can probably tour in an afternoon stroll, will be overwhelmed by the size and scope of the San Diego Zoo. The zoo is home to over 4,000 animals representing 800 species; although the classic zoo animals your children expect to see are present and accounted for, you'll also meet giant pandas, koalas, kiwis, and takins.

Details

In Balboa Park, off Park Boulevard, San Diego
619-234-3153

The zoo, which is located only minutes from downtown San Diego, is open daily from 9 A.M. to 4 P.M. off-season and until 9 P.M. from mid-June to Labor Day. It's essential to come early because it will take a full day to tour the grounds, and families who enter at noon will be too busy fighting the heat and the crowds to see much. Admission is $15 for adults, $6 for kids 3 to 11; the bus tour is an additional $4 for adults, $3 for kids; the Kangaroo Bus costs $8 and $5 if purchased separately. A combination ticket to the zoo and the San Diego Wild Animal Park costs $32.95 for adults, $19.35 for kids 3 to 11. Call for directions and other details.

Highlights

The best bets in the zoo include the "bioclimatic zones," which are special exhibits located within botanical gardens where mist machines, heated caves, and even the piped-in sounds of tropical birds are combined to simulate the natural habitat of the animal being exhibited. It's the ability to re-create these native environments that sets the San Diego Zoo apart from the rest. Featured are Tiger River (a humid Asian rain forest with Sumatran tigers, tapirs, and Chinese water dragons), Sun Bear Forest (a sunny rock pile where the Malaysian sun bears frolic), Gorilla Tropics (an African jungle complete with waterfalls, vines, and a huge troop of lowland gorillas), and Pygmy Chimps (a walking trail through streams and palms where the friendly chimps do amazing acrobatics). Visit at least one of the natural habitats.

Don't miss the 20-minute Wild Ones Show, where trained animals and birds not seen anywhere else in the zoo perform antics and special tricks.

Possibly the most popular zoo attraction is the Giant Panda Exhibit. The zoo is rigorous about making sure the pandas are seen only at certain times and that the viewers (who are moved along quickly) keep their voices down. If your kids are really determined to see the pandas, be sure to call the Panda Hotline (888-MY PANDA) toll free to find out what the viewing times are that day.

If your kids are younger than 8, save time for the Children's Zoo. Although we found this the least impressive area of the zoo, there's no doubting that kids are mad for petting zoos. Domestic animals, such as sheep, pigs, and goats, roam the grounds with their more exotic compatriots. But the real stars are the infant monkeys and tigers that live in the glass-fronted nursery. Even the most cynical zoo-goer can't help but coo at the sight of the babies with their diapers and bottles. At various times throughout the day, there are animal presentations in small, intimate settings. This way the youngsters can better "meet" the different species and learn more about them.

Touring Tips

• Be at the entrance gate about 8:45 A.M. Once in the park, walk through Tiger River while everyone's still energetic, then move on to the bus tour. The 35-minute, three-mile guided bus tour gives you a good introduction to the layout of the zoo. You'll see a fair amount from the double-decker buses—but the main advantage to the tour is that it helps you decide what you want to come back to later. The best views are from the second level of the bus, so queue up even though the lines for the top are always longer. There is no way for even the most fleet-footed family to see everything at the San Diego Zoo, so make sure what you do see is the best. The most popular sights with our group were the pandas, koalas, elephants, seals, and gorillas.

• Although the bus tour is a good idea, you can't jump off when the kids yell, "I want to see that elephant!" If you think you'll want to get on and off, take the Kangaroo Bus instead. It's still a guided tour, but you can get on and off at eight designated stops for a better look, and you can ride it all day.

• Be careful—there's a lot of walking required to tour the zoo, and some sections, most notably the Horn and Hoof Mesa, can wear you out fast. It's better to see fewer exhibits and give the kids time to really enjoy the animals than to rush about in a frenzied and doomed effort to see it all. One strategy is to skip the zebras, giraffes, and other animals you're likely to see in any zoo and concentrate on the more unusual animals.

• Because the zoo is so large and hilly, never walk when there's a way to ride. Consult your map and use the Skyfari aerial tramway and people-mover stairways to get around, especially when going uphill.

• In the afternoon when everyone's stamina begins to flag, rest up at one of the shows or leave the zoo and roam around Balboa Park for an hour or two. With its museums, playgrounds, train, and wide-open spaces, the park is a fun destination in itself. Several of the zoo's fast-food places offer sandwiches, salads, children's boxed meals, and other easily transported food, so you can eat in the park. The Children's Zoo, which has several play areas, is also a good option when you sense you've gone one llama too far.

• Don't forget that some of the cats, like the snow leopard, are nocturnal. In summer, nighttime at the zoo becomes very special. Those nocturnal animals, and others such as tigers, lions, fruit bats, and more, "wake up." This is a great opportunity for the kids to see animals doing what comes naturally. There's also a laser show in summer, along with storytellers and other entertainers. Consider an evening visit with dinner at the zoo.

SAN DIEGO WILD ANIMAL PARK

This wonderful park is not a zoo—instead, the animals basically run free while visitors circle their habitats by monorail. The five-mile, 55-minute loop around the park provides a quick introduction to the more than 3,000 animals in residence. The sight of these creatures in such a huge, open space can be breathtaking; you may see a dozen giraffes moving as one across the savannah, a mother rhino charging a male that got too close to her 800-pound baby, or a pride of lions napping impassively in the sun.

What sets this tour apart is the sincerity of the guides, who feel strongly about the park's commitment to saving endangered species and really care about what they're doing. The San Diego Zoo and Wild Animal Park team has single-handedly brought several species back from the brink of extinction.

Details

15500 San Pasqual Valley Road, Escondido
760-234-6541

Some people think the San Diego Zoo and Wild Animal Park are right next to each other. Actually, the Wild Animal Park is about 35 miles north of San Diego in Escondido. It's open every day of the year from 9 A.M. Closing times vary.

Admission is $19.95 for adults, $12.95 for kids 3 to 11. A combination ticket for the park and the San Diego Zoo is $32.95 for adults, $19.35 for kids.

Highlights

Wgasa Bush Line is the centerpiece of the Wild Animal Park and very popular, so you must go early or face major waits. The right-hand side of the monorail has the best views, but because riders are allowed to stand, everyone on board can see. The two drawbacks of the monorail ride are that you're quite a distance away from the animals and you can't linger with the species you find most interesting. But the park's shows, Kilimanjaro walking path, and Heart of Africa remedy this problem. There's also a small petting kraal in Nairobi Village, where baby animals are brought out and bottle-fed. Check times at the Animal Care Center.

The Bird Show, the Elephant Show, and Rare and Wild America are best seen in the afternoon after you've taken the monorail ride. The Wild Animal Park also features a number of walk-through exhibits, such as Lorikeet Landing, where you can feed cups of nectar to the bold Australian birds and get closer to everything from butterflies to gorillas.

The tours and classes offered by the San Diego Wild Animal Park are unparalleled. If your children are older than 12, consider taking one of the Photo Caravan Safaris, which transport parties of about 12 people (loaded onto the back of a flatbed truck) into the heart of the large animal exhibits. Rhinos, zebras, and giraffes will come right up to the side of the truck, and you'll be able to reach down, touch them, feed them, and, of course, get wonderful pictures. You'll get the type of contact with the animals that is impossible in any other zoo, and your personal guide is prepared to go into far more detail than you'd get on the monorail ride. The Photo Caravans run Wednesday through Sunday year-round; they're extremely popular, so advance reservations are a must, at least two weeks in advance. For reservations, call 760-738-5022. The two-hour tour is $65; the three-and-a-half-hour tour is $89, with admission to the park included in the price. Expensive, yes, but for a young person with a real interest in animal life, it's a once-in-a-lifetime opportunity.

The Photo Caravans are not the only educational opportunities offered, and the Wild Animal Park is always fine-tuning its programs. Check with the park for current programs by calling 760-738-5057.

As the Wild Animal Park is an hour away from San Diego, trying to see both in the same day is impossible. Devote a different day to each attraction, perhaps breaking them up a bit with a trip to the beach or Sea World.

On a tight touring schedule? If you can see only one, let the ages of your children be the determining factor. The zoo appeals more to kids younger than 7 because often they need to get close to the animals to appreciate them. But kids older than 7, who likely have already visited conventional zoos, may prefer the Wild Animal Park because the animals are showcased in a truly unique way. Whichever you choose, you won't be disappointed.

Attractions

Once you've seen the vast panorama offered on the monorail, visit the Kilimanjaro Safari Walk. This hiking trail will take you closer to some of those beasties you saw on the monorail. It will also lead you to the backcountry portion of park. This is a part of the park you won't see on the monorail.

All ages will get something out of the newest experience called the Heart of Africa. The Wild Animal Park has attempted to re-create a true African safari within a 30-acre setting. The trail through the Heart of Africa is about three quarters of a mile long and is accessible to strollers. The point is to explore the changing terrain with no barriers between you and the animals and birds. Of course there are barriers, but this is one of the only places where you can be as close as 10 feet to some of the critters. You can even feed the giraffes! A mock research island is occupied by "researchers" who describe what it would be like to actually live and work in the heart of Africa. With the help of the professionals, the kids can meet even more animals. If you walk it leisurely, the Heart of Africa shouldn't take more than an hour.

Touring Tips

• Be at the park a little before 9 A.M. After the gates open, head straight to the monorail. The monorail is the only attraction to draw long lines, so it's best to ride it early in the day. Early is also preferable as many animals take a snooze midday—a good time for the human characters to grab lunch.

• The 55-minute ride makes no stops, so visit the bathroom before you board. You can push a stroller through the winding line right up to the monorail, and the driver will bring you back to it after the tour is completed, even though other passengers disembark elsewhere.

• The Wild Animal Park can be toured in four to five hours. Because it is located between Los Angeles and San Diego and can be toured relatively quickly, it makes a good final stop on the day you commute between the two cities.

Tip: Because the park isn't overwhelmingly huge, it's also a good choice to tour in late afternoon and evening on the nights it's open late. On Thursday through Sunday during the summer, the park stays open until 10 P.M., although the gates close at 8 P.M.

• The Kilimanjaro Trail, which leads past animal exhibits into the gardens, is fun to explore in the afternoon. The walk is brief but hilly, and you'll have to keep toddlers on the path because only a few feet from the concrete lies rocky terrain—and very possibly critters. Don't attempt to travel the whole trail with a stroller or climb to the top where the gardens are; if your kids are young, stay in the open area at the beginning of the trail.

• The shows are another good choice for the afternoon, especially the elephants. Then explore the petting kraal and the exhibits and restaurants of Nairobi Village. Be sure to hit the gift shops on your way out—the T-shirt and toy selections here are outstanding.

• Because of the size of the Heart of Africa, explore this one before the youngsters get too tired. Morning and early evening are good because the animals are awake then.

• Kilima Point is a great photo spot.

WHERE TO STAY IN SAN DIEGO

There is a wide array of accommodations to choose from: Mission Bay is a great place to stay with youngsters, La Jolla's beaches are superb, and Coronado is a getaway of its own. Places to stay range from the luxury of the one-of-a-kind Hotel del Coronado to budget chains such as Days' Inn.

For a complete guide to the variety of area hotels, call or write:

San Diego Convention and Visitors Bureau
401 B Street, Suite 1400
Dept. 700
San Diego, CA 92101-4237
619-232-1212

In addition to accommodations, the guide includes discount coupons for restaurants, hotels, and admissions to some of the most popular sights. Various discount hotel clubs list a variety of area hotels offering discounts that can bring the rates down substantially. Weekends during summers and holidays get booked quickly. Be sure to plan your visit in advance and, when possible, take advantage of discounted weekend rates off-season.

Here are some of the best accommodations for families. They're not cheap, but if you can afford it, they're worth the splurge.

San Diego Yacht and Breakfast Company

Marina Cortez, Harbor Island
800-YACHT DO (800-922-4836)

This is possibly the most unique of the following accommodations. It's just what the name says—guests rent a yacht or "villa" docked at the marina in Harbor Island and get a daily breakfast. The breakfasts aren't elaborate, but they fill you up. You also get a discount card for restaurants in the immediate area, and there's a pool for guest use.

The "villas" are well-appointed houseboats that are permanently docked at Marina Cortez. The one-bedroom houseboat is perfect for a family of four. The private "stateroom" has a queen-size bed, its own TV, and a bath with shower (there's a second bathroom). The living room features a queen-size sofa bed, table and chairs, answering machine, TV, stereo, VCR, and disc player. The kitchen is fully stocked, and there's a microwave and coffeemaker along with a full-size refrigerator and stove; there's even a washer and dryer! A tiny veranda off the living room leads to a patio on the upper deck that is perfect for a bird's-eye view of the marina and the gorgeous boats. There's little motion on the houseboat, but you'll still get that nautical feeling. The two-bedroom houseboat sleeps six and has a redwood hot tub on the upper deck. The "villas" go for $225 to $295 per night. Each extra person is $25.

Or you can really splurge and rent a 41- or 51-foot yacht that tours the San Diego Bay with a captain. One family from Scotland stayed on the smaller yacht for two weeks and took it out once. It sleeps four, has two full baths, and rents for from $225 nightly. To take it out for a three-hour Bay trip with a captain, you'll pay another $100 per hour. The larger yacht can sleep six (with a pullout) and has a bigger salon and aft stateroom. This one rents for $345. Both boats are fully stocked and well taken care of.

Kids under age 5 aren't allowed in either the villas or the yachts, and you're encouraged to take children of ages that can be trusted around water. Remember that all you have to do is step off your boat and there's water everywhere.

Keep in mind the following: You'll be asked for a hefty returnable deposit to ensure there's no damage to the boats. There's no maid service (although the accommodations have plenty of extra towels and sheets). If you plan to check in after 9 P.M., be sure to let them know that in advance. In summer months, they're booked four to five months in advance. There's a nonrefundable deposit of one night's fee and final payment to be made 30 days in advance.

Even if you don't arrange for a captain to take you out, you can rent water "toys"—like sailboats and skiffs—at a discount. Here's a tip: One night, call the Water Taxi, which will pick you up at the Marina and drop you anywhere on San Diego Bay for about $5. But be sure to call them well in advance, especially on weekends, as there's only one taxi.

The Hotel del Coronado

1500 Orange Avenue, Coronado
800-HOTEL DEL or 619-522-8000

The beautiful "Del," as it is known, is a National Historic Landmark that is famous for its guests (for example, Franklin Roosevelt and Ronald Reagan) and is the spot where Wallis Simpson and the Prince of Wales first met. In addition to being interesting from a historic perspective, the "Del" has a great children's program. There are also planned family activities, great facilities, a spectacular beachfront, and a large, interesting retail arcade. Rates run around $215 to $525. Kids sleep free.

Loews Coronado Bay Resort

4000 Coronado Bay Road, Coronado
800-815-6397 or 619-424-4000

Not far from the "Del," the Loews is another top-notch spot for families. It's a European-like hotel with a children's program, special holiday activities, and summer family programs. There are five tennis courts and a health club and three pools (two of them are designated for families). Rates begin at $195, but there are numerous packages to inquire about.

As mentioned before, Mission Bay is a great place to stay with young children. Two resorts stand out here. My favorite is the San Diego Hilton.

San Diego Hilton Beach and Tennis Resort

> 1775 East Mission Bay Drive, San Diego
> 800-HILTONS or 619-276-4010

The recreation and pool area is spacious; the pool is huge, and there's a separate wading pool for toddlers. The hotel is on the shore and convenient to a bike path (bikes can be rented); kids can play in the sand, and you can rent water-sport equipment. There's also a summer children's program, plus special activities for adults. If you rent one of the first-floor garden rooms, your sliding glass doors will open directly on to large grassy areas perfect for playing. It's not far to the beach from these rooms. Rates here start at $220 in summer season, and kids sleep free.

San Diego Princess

> 1404 West Vacation Road, San Diego
> 800-344-2626 or 619-274-4630

Many parents traditionally return year after year to the San Diego Princess, also located on Mission Bay and close to Sea World. There are a variety of accommodations here, including studios that open up directly to the beach and that sleep five. Some of these have cooking facilities. This self-contained resort features six swimming pools and has a little self-guided botanical tour, bridges, bike rentals, and its own marina. Room rates range from $140 to $365, and kids under 12 are free. (Ask about special promotional rates.)

WHERE TO EAT IN SAN DIEGO

Restaurants in San Diego are plentiful, and because the area is so family oriented, you won't have much trouble finding a spot for a casual meal.

• Planet Hollywood in Horton Plaza downtown (619-702-7827) is good if you have preteens and teens in tow.

• The Hard Rock Café in La Jolla (619-456-7625) is also a good choice for preteens and teens.

• Islands, also in La Jolla, is great for kids who like hamburgers (619-455-9945).

• The Mexican restaurants in Bazaar del Mundo (Old Town) are comfortable and colorful and great for any age-group.

• The San Diego Pier Café in Seaport Village is the place to go if you want a view of the bay. Call 619-239-3968 to make a reservation. Children's menus are provided.

CHAPTER *11*

Making the Trip
Educational

"Educational" may not be the first word that comes to mind when you think of taking a trip to Southern California. But among the beaches, roller coasters, and movie stars, there are plenty of opportunities to learn new things. Kids remember what they see and do long after they forget what they hear and read, so all travel has the potential to be educational. The trick is presenting the experience in a way that's age-appropriate for the child.

The following attractions have the most educational potential:

Sea World
San Diego Zoo
San Diego Wild Animal Park
Catalina Island (especially the nature tours)
Whale-watching
Leo Carillo Beach
Los Angeles Zoo
Griffith Observatory (in Griffith Park)
NBC Studio Tour
Paramount Studio Tour
Warner Bros. VIP Tour

Any of the museums including:

The Getty Center
Los Angeles Children's Museum
La Brea Tar Pits (at the George C. Page Museum)
Natural History Museum
Peterson Automotive Museum
Museum of Flying
Autry Museum of Western Heritage
The California Science Center

If the kids are old enough to be studying popular culture or the media, Los Angeles will serve as the ultimate lab. Some of the best post-trip school reports have come from the unlikely area of Hollywood: One teenage girl traced the history of how women have been portrayed in films, providing starlet photos she picked up at a sleazy Hollywood souvenir shop to illustrate her points. A 14-year-old boy, interested in the more technical end of moviemaking, used the family camcorder to mimic the moves of the studio camera he observed during the NBC studio tour. Once home, he practiced film editing for the first time, with predictably vertigo-producing results, and turned his documentary "Luke Does L.A." into a social studies project.

To help your kids get the most out of the trip, here are some tips to remember:

- Consider taking the guided tours. They not only get you closer to the action but also give you access to an expert—someone who can explain just what the difference between a sea lion and a seal really is. The tours at Sea World, the San Diego Zoo, the San Diego Wild Animal Park, and Catalina Island are obviously educational, but don't forget the behind-the-scenes tour at Disneyland. Although much of the tour is geared toward trivia, it also strips back the fantasy and shows you how this huge machine known as Disneyland works. The logistics of costuming, crowd control, setting up the parades and shows, moving around food and merchandise, and even security are fascinating, and the tour gives you some sense of the science behind the magic.

To take most of the tours, you'll need to make arrangements in advance by calling Guest Relations at the park you'll be visiting. Some tours, like those at Sea World, run frequently and can be reserved with a day's notice; others, like the Photo Caravan Safaris at the San Diego Wild Animal Park, sell out months in advance.

• Taking the kids out of school for the trip? Speak with their teachers in advance about special projects they can do for class credit. If the subject is one that doesn't easily lend itself to outside projects, like math or spelling, see if they can do at least some of the work they'll be missing before you go. Coming back from a vacation to piles of makeup work can be profoundly depressing.

In other subjects—history, science, geography, and English—you should be able to agree on a project to research during your trip. Young kids might simply make a leaf collection to show how West Coast trees differ from East Coast trees. Older children might wish to start with a thesis (like the girl who noticed how differently women are portrayed in movies than men) and collect data throughout the trip to prove or disprove the thesis. A trip journal (described following) can often combine several subjects.

• Create some sort of journal or scrapbook to commemorate your trip. Younger kids might want to trace their route on a map, using their math skills to calculate mileage traveled, make a montage from postcards and brochures, or use a portable tape recorder to interview a tour guide or expert.

An idea that's both simple and clever for kids younger than 7 is to buy a postcard at each stop and let the child dictate to the parent what was most memorable about the place. The parent writes the child's observations on the back of the postcard, then punches a hole in the top of the card and puts it on a metal ring (the sort you can find in any stationery store). By the trip's end the child has a sequential flip chart of the places she's visited and what she liked best about each. This is not only a priceless souvenir but also a great thing to take to school for show-and-tell.

If you do have your preschool child dictate a diary, try to resist the temptation to edit her observations. Children frequently notice different things than adults do, and if your daughter's most vivid memory of the San Diego Zoo is the cool green soap in the bathroom dispenser, then so be it. The diaries are much more meaningful in the long run if you use the child's own words.

Older children can obviously keep their own travel records, and a trip log can include information about science, history, and geography and give the child the chance to sharpen his writing skills. The addition of photos makes the journal more enticing.

• In planning a school project, it helps to narrow your focus. Heading to Sea World to do a report on "Marine Life" is too broad, but "Penguins" would be perfect. Don't overwhelm the kid with a topic too big to cover.

• It's also important to broaden your definitions. If you think of history as Civil War battlefields, you're missing the chance to turn more recent events into reports. Television shows and movies are valid indicators of an era's values as well. It doesn't have to be ancient to be historic.

Science can likewise be fun—why not study earthquakes or dinosaurs or how dolphins are trained? The question, "How did they do that?" innocently asked after a show or ride, can lead to interesting answers.

• Have your child read up on California before the trip. A biography of Walt Disney, a history of the Gold Rush, or a John Steinbeck novel will give your student things to think about before you even board the plane.

There are a number of fiction books set in Southern California appropriate for teenagers: "Island of the Blue Dolphin" is one of the best.

Perhaps a better name for this chapter would be "*Letting* the Trip Be Educational." The best learning opportunities aren't forced or contrived, as in "Get up, Jennifer, we're going to do something . . . (drum roll) . . . educational today," but rather seem to arise naturally out of the situation. Under the right conditions, the child's own curiosity will drive him, and because many kids view learning as a passive (not active) experience, he probably won't even be aware that he is learning.

INDEX

Florida with Kids
1998–1999

Bill McMillon

U.S. $14.95 / Can. $19.95
ISBN 0-7615-0474-5
paperback / 320 pages

Walt Disney World is, undoubtedly, Florida's main family tourist attraction, drawing millions of visitors every year. But what if you're looking for something off the beaten path? Noted travel writer Bill McMillon guides readers through Florida's seven major regions, providing an organized look at the overwhelming variety of things to do and see in the Sunshine State. This helpful handbook offers

many tips for keeping your kids amused—and you relaxed. Inside you'll find listings of educational and historic sites and museums as well as a guide to 180 of the best family-friendly restaurants, hotels, motels, and campgrounds.

To order, call (800) 632-8676 or
visit us online at www.primapublishing.com

Walt Disney World® with Kids, 1998

Kim Wright Wiley

U.S. $14.00 / Can. $18.95
ISBN 0-7615-0808-2
paperback / 368 pages

Millions of families travel to Walt Disney World every year, but even "the happiest place on earth" can be exhausting and expensive without a knowledgeable guide. Author Kim Wright Wiley to the rescue! The nation's leading expert on traveling to Walt Disney World with kids in tow, she tells parents how to plan a wonderful, carefree vacation the kids will never forget with tips on the best hotels and restaurants for kids, smart ways to beat the crowds, and ratings for the most kid-pleasing rides.

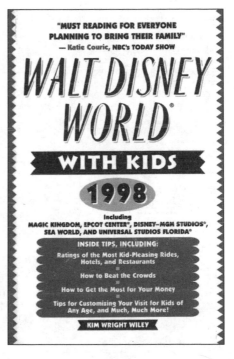

To order, call (800) 632-8676 or visit us online at www.primapublishing.com

To Order Books

Please send me the following items:

Quantity	Title	Unit Price	Total
_____	Florida with Kids, 1998–1999	$ 14.95	$ _____
_____	Walt Disney World with Kids, 1998	$ 14.00	$ _____
_____	_____	$ _____	$ _____
_____	_____	$ _____	$ _____
_____	_____	$ _____	$ _____

*Shipping and Handling depend on Subtotal.

Subtotal	Shipping/Handling
$0.00–$14.99	$3.00
$15.00–$29.99	$4.00
$30.00–$49.99	$6.00
$50.00–$99.99	$10.00
$100.00–$199.99	$13.50
$200.00+	Call for Quote

Foreign and all Priority Request orders:
Call Order Entry department
for price quote at 916-632-4400

This chart represents the total retail price of books only (before applicable discounts are taken).

Subtotal $ _____
Deduct 10% when ordering 3–5 books $ _____
7.25% Sales Tax (CA only) $ _____
8.25% Sales Tax (TN only) $ _____
5% Sales Tax (MD and IN only) $ _____
7% G.S.T. Tax (Canada only) $ _____
Shipping and Handling* $ _____
Total Order $ _____

By Telephone: With MC, American Express, or Visa, call 800-632-8676 or 916-632-4400. Mon–Fri, 8:30-4:30.

WWW: http://www.primapublishing.com

By Internet E-mail: sales@primapub.com

By Mail: Just fill out the information below and send with your remittance to:

**Prima Publishing
P.O. Box 1260BK
Rocklin, CA 95677**

Name _____

Address_____

City _____ State _____ ZIP_____

MC/Visa#_____ Exp. _____

Check/money order enclosed for $_____ Payable to Prima Publishing

Daytime telephone _____

Signature _____